P. Hewitt

Klett Sicher in Englisch

Grammatik 9./10. Klasse

Alles zum Thema Grammatik

Klett Lerntraining

Hinweis:
Zu diesem Buch gehören Online-Tests unter
www.klasse5bis10.klett-lerntraining.de.
Der Zugang zu den Online-Abschlusstests ist bis drei Jahre nach Ersterscheinen des Buches gewährleistet.

Dieses Werk basiert auf 978-3-12-927533-7.

Bibliografische Information der Deutschen Nationalbibliothek
Die Deutsche Nationalbibliothek verzeichnet diese Publikation in der Deutschen Nationalbibliografie; detaillierte bibliografische Daten sind im Internet über http://dnb.dnb.de abrufbar.

3. Auflage 2025

www.klett-lerntraining.de/kontakt
Cover: Rücken Shutterstock (Sazhnieva Oksana), New York; U1/U4 Getty Images (pixdeluxe), München
Lektorat: Joanne Popp, editing etc., Korntal-Münchingen
Satz: DTP-Studio Andrea Eckhardt, Göppingen
Druck: Multiprint Ltd., Kostinbrod
Printed in Bulgaria
ISBN 978-3-12-927627-3

Inhaltsverzeichnis

4 Bedingungssätze

5 Die indirekte Rede

6 Partizipien – Gerundium – Infinitiv

7 Das Passiv

8 Modale Hilfsverben

9 Relativsätze

Lösungen

So übst du mit diesem Buch

Du möchtest sicher in der englischen Grammatik werden?
Dann ist dieses Buch genau das richtige Übungsbuch für dich! Es hilft dir dabei, alle **wichtigen Themen** der englischen Grammatik zu wiederholen und zu üben.

Gehe so vor:

Schritt 1

Suche aus dem Inhaltsverzeichnis das **Thema heraus**, das du wiederholen möchtest.

Schritt 2

Lies das **Merkwissen** im Kasten **durch**. Dort steht alles, was du zu diesem Thema wissen und können solltest.

Schritt 3

Jetzt kannst du mit den vielen unterschiedlichen **Aufgaben üben**. Einige Aufgaben lassen sich aus Platzgründen nicht im Buch lösen – lege dir dafür Papier bereit.

Schritt 4

Vergleiche deine Antworten mit den **Lösungen** hinten im Buch.

Schritt 5

Wenn du ein Kapitel abgeschlossen hast, kannst du dich mit dem **Abschlusstest online testen**. Die Ergebnisse aus dem Test kannst du in die Tabelle am Kapitelende übertragen. So behältst du immer den Überblick.

So funktioniert der Abschlusstest online

Gehe auf www.klett-lerntraining.de/5X7F.

Du erhältst eine Übersicht über alle Kapitel und darunter alle verfügbaren Abschlusstests.
Wähle einen passenden Test aus und bearbeite die Aufgaben.

Du kannst alle Online-Tests mit und ohne Anmeldung nutzen.
Bitte beachte: Wenn du dich nicht anmeldest, kann dein Lernstand in den Tests **nicht gespeichert** werden.

Eine Anmeldung ist nur möglich, wenn du dich vorher bei uns registriert hast. Dafür musst du dir einen Benutzernamen und ein Passwort ausdenken und deine E-Mail-Adresse angeben. Dann erhältst du einen Aktivierungslink per E-Mail.

Informationen zu Registrierung und Anmeldung findest du immer unter „**Hilfe**" in unserem Lernportal www.klasse5bis10.klett-lerntraining.de.

Viel Erfolg wünschen dir die Autoren und das Team von Klett-Lerntraining

1 Adjektiv und Adverb

1.1 Die Unterschiede zwischen Adjektiv und Adverb

Adjektive beschreiben Nomen. Sie stehen entweder

- direkt vor dem Nomen.
  › She drives a **fast** car.
- als Ergänzung hauptsächlich nach *to be*, *to get*, *to become*.
  › He is **silly**.
  Our teacher got **angry**.

Adjektive werden auch mit *the* benutzt, um bestimmte Gruppen (vor allem von Personen) zu bezeichnen.

› The **poor** get poorer and the **rich** get richer.
We are collecting money for the **blind**.

Adverbien (meist Adjektiv + *-ly*) beschreiben

1. Verben.
   › She drives **badly**.
2. Adjektive.
   › She is **extremely** clever.
   We were **very** angry.
3. andere Adverbien.
   › She speaks **terribly** quickly.

Einige wichtige Adverbien haben Formen ohne *-ly*.

- Adverbien, die Adjektive oder andere Adverbien beschreiben, wie z.B. *very*, *too*, *far*, *much*.
  › It's **very** expensive.
- Adverbien wie z.B. *hard*, *long*, *high*, *low*, *deep*, *fast*.

Von Adjektiven, die bereits mit *-ly* enden, wird eine Umschreibung benutzt.

› A friendly person smiles **in a friendly way**.

Aufgabe 1

a) Read the following text and list the adverbs used in the three categories (with verbs, adjectives or other adverbs) given in the rules on page 8.

b) Then list all the adjectives used.

The last frontier

Graham Hawkes designed a revolutionary new submarine which was lowered gently into the waters of Monterey Bay for its first voyage. Deep Flight I is shaped like a torpedo but flies faster than other deep-sea research vessels. The pilot, who lies inside the vessel with his or her head in the glass nose, can move as fast as the fastest whale or even leap vertically out of the sea.

More than 100 expeditions have reached the top of Everest, the world's highest mountain, and manned voyages into space have become common. But it is only now that the deepest parts of the ocean are gradually being explored. Sylvia Earle, a co-founder of the company which built Deep Flight I, said, "We know much more about Mars than we know about the ocean floor."

Although scientists are most interested in exploring the deepest parts of the ocean, little is known about the middle waters five to six kilometres down, or even the "shallows" just 100 metres below the surface of the sea.

The oceans are the world's last great frontier. They easily contain more life by weight than any other ecosystem, and their economic potential is equally great. Majestically moving ocean currents influence much of the world's weather. If we can find out how they operate, we could save billions of dollars in weather-related disasters.

The seas contain many valuable minerals and other substances. "The discoveries helpful to mankind will far outweigh those of the space program," says Bruce Robinson of the Monterey Bay Aquarium Research Institute, California. "If we can get to the bottom of the sea fairly regularly, mankind will benefit immediately."

Aufgabe 2

Put the right forms of the words in brackets in the following sentences.

1. In 1960 the deep-sea submarine *Trieste* was ________________ **(careful)** lowered to a depth of 10,912 metres.
2. On board the *Trieste* were two __________ **(brave)** scientists.
3. The deep-sea submarine behaved __________ **(good)**.
4. Unlike the ____________________ **(complicated)** vehicles used today, the *Trieste* contained __________ **(only)** the passengers.
5. They went down ____________________ **(slow/very)**.
6. They reached the bottom ___________ **(safe)**.
7. They knew that people would __________ **(soon)** be able to explore the depths of the oceans.
8. After the *Trieste's* dive, the number of deep-sea submarines increased ________________ **(dramatic)**.
9. The __________ **(old)** American three-person submarine *Alvin*, launched in 1964, is still operating.
10. The first ROVs, vehicles _____________ **(remote)** operated from the surface, followed _____________ **(quick)**.
11. These were equipped with _________________ **(expensive)** cameras and collecting equipment.
12. Some were built for the army, but others were designed for __________________ **(scientific)** research.
13. At last ___________ **(marine)** biologists could collect samples.
14. A __________________ **(complete)** new era of scientific research had begun.

15. Until then, geologists only had an ______________________________ **(imperfect)** basic knowledge of the sea bed.

16. They know now that the sea floor is not an ______________ **(endless)**, flat plain stretching from continent to continent.

17. Rocks from the sea bed, when ______________ **(close)** examined, were found to contain valuable minerals.

18. The new deep-sea submarines can dive ______________________________ ______________________________ **(deep/astonishing)**!

Aufgabe 3

Here is an unusual crossword puzzle. Follow the arrows to finish the sentences. Use adjectives or adverbs as required. Here are some but not all the words you need: useful, awful, first, unhappy, full, loud, well. You will have to guess the others from the context.

Down:
1. Mr Smith is a very … worker. He gets a lot of work done.
2. How are you today? – I'm very …, thank you.
3. He isn't a fast reader. He reads quite … .
4. The music was very … . I couldn't hear myself speak.
7. Is that the answer? Are you …?
9. … marks if you get all the answers right!
11. … weather today, isn't it? It hasn't stopped raining.
12. We got up … to drive to the airport.

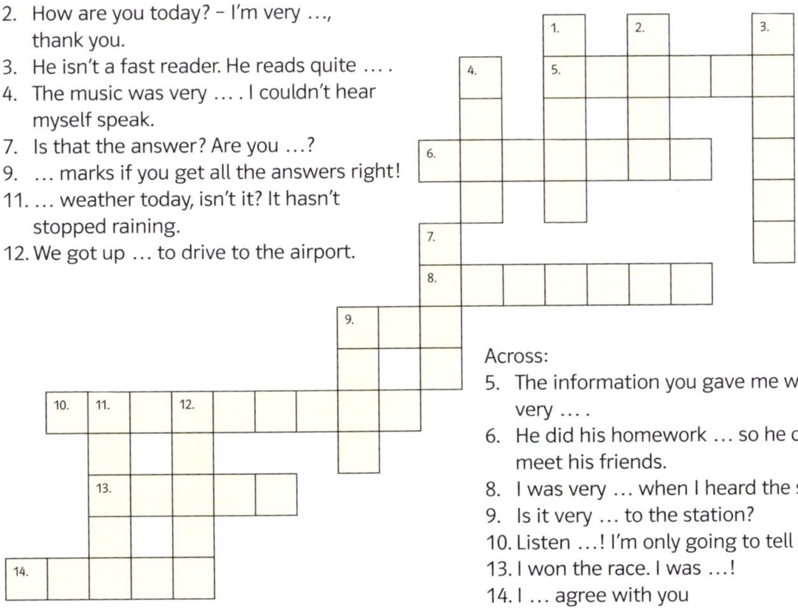

Across:
5. The information you gave me was very … .
6. He did his homework … so he could meet his friends.
8. I was very … when I heard the sad news.
9. Is it very … to the station?
10. Listen …! I'm only going to tell you once.
13. I won the race. I was …!
14. I … agree with you

1.2 Die Steigerung von Adjektiven und Adverbien

Adjektive

Einsilbige **Adjektive** werden mit den Endungen *-er*, *-est* gesteigert.

› This car is older than ours.
It's the oldest car in the street.

Nach kurzem Vokal wird ein einzelner Konsonant verdoppelt.

› It's a big house – bigger than I thought!

End *-e* verschmilzt mit der Endung; *-y* wird zu *-i* vor der Endung.

› 2018 was the finest and driest summer in Britain for 300 years.

Zweisilbige Adjektive mit sehr kurzer zweiter Silbe (*-y*, *-ow*, *-le*, *-er*) nehmen auch die Endungen *-er*, *-est* an.

› We're happier now.
He is cleverer than me.

Alle anderen zwei- und mehrsilbigen Adjektive werden durch Anfügung von *more* und (*the*) *most* gesteigert.

› This car is more modern and more comfortable than your old one.
I think it's the most modern and most comfortable car I've ever travelled in.

Adverbien

Einsilbige **Adverbien** werden mit den Endungen *-er*, *-est* gesteigert.

› She runs faster than me.
John works quicker.

Es gelten die gleichen Rechtschreibregeln wie für Adjektive.

› We arrived later than Mia.
Max arrived latest/last of all, as usual!

Die meisten Adverbien werden mit der Endung *-ly* vom Adjektiv gebildet und haben deshalb zwei Silben. Sie werden mit *more* und (*the*) *most* gesteigert.

› You must drive more carefully.
Of all the drivers I know, she drives the most carefully.

Eine „negative" Steigerung kann man mit *less* und *least* ausdrücken.

› This book is less interesting than the last one I read.

She worked less hard last term.

Unregelmäßige Steigerungen von Adjektiven und Adverbien:

good	– better	– best		well	– better	– best
bad	– worse	– worst		much	– more	– most
many/much	– more	– most		badly	– worse	– worst
little	– less	– least		little	– less	– least

Aufgabe 4

Put the right form of the word in brackets in the following sentences.

1. **(good)**

   "Do you know a ______________ snack bar? A place where they cook really ______________?" – "Have you tried McDouglas's? It's ______________ than McSweeny's. I think it's the ______________ place in town."

2. **(bad)**

   "Well, it can't be ______________ than McDougall's. My sister Sue says they make the ______________ salads in London." – "How is your sister Sue?" – "She's not doing ______________. She's got a new job."

3. **(interesting)**

   "She says it's much ______________ than her old one."

4. **(happy)**

   "I thought she was ______________ in her old job." – "Well, she's ______________ in this new job. She says the people who work there are the ______________ people she's ever worked with. By the way, how are you getting on at school?" – "I'm not very ______________ with my progress."

→

5. **(difficult)**

"You're learning Italian now, aren't you? Do you find it ______________ than French?" – "No, it's ______________ than French. I think French is the ______________ language I have ever tried to learn!"

6. **(much)**

"I don't have ______________ time for sports now. I had ______________ time last year. I don't have as ______________ money either." – "You have too ______________ hobbies! You should organise your time ______________ carefully."

7. **(little)**

"Most parents have ______________ time to talk to their children than for watching TV." – "I don't know. My mum only has a ______________ time for TV. She watches TV ______________ than my dad. I think she watches the ______________ TV of us all!"

8. **(good/bad)**

"Do you feel ______________ today?" – "I feel ______________ than I felt yesterday." – "Don't you think it would be ______________ to stay in bed?" – "No. I can work ______________ on the sofa." – "I've got exams in three weeks! I must do ______________ this year because I did so ______________ last year. They were my ______________ exams ever!" – "You'd ______________ speak to the doctor. You won't do ______________ if you're ill. Your results will be ______________ than last year's!"

9. **(extreme)**

"I don't like our headmaster. He has ______________ views on education." – "He's ______________ strict, I know. But I don't think he's ______________ than most headmasters." – "Well, he's the ______________ headmaster I've ever met!"

1.3 Die Stellung von Adverbien im Satz

1. **Am Satzanfang** stehen
   - Zeitbestimmungen.
     › **On Mondays** we go swimming.
   - Ortsbestimmungen, die betont werden.
     › **In London** (not in Birmingham) people speak a dialect called Cockney.
   - Einwort-Adverbien, die sich auf den ganzen Satz beziehen.
     › **Unfortunately** we can do nothing to help you.

2. **Am Satz- oder Satzteilende** stehen
   - Ortsbestimmungen.
     › On Mondays we go swimming **in the open-air swimming pool**.
   - Zeitbestimmungen.
     › We go swimming **on Mondays**.
     Enthält ein Satz zwei Zeitadverbien, steht die genauere Zeitbestimmung meist am Satzende.
     › **Next year** she's visiting New York **in the spring**.
   - Orts- und Zeitbestimmungen.
     Im Gegensatz zum Deutschen steht **ORT vor ZEIT**.
     We're going **to Leipzig tomorrow evening**.
     (*vgl.: Wir fahren* ***morgen Abend nach Leipzig****.*)

3. **Vor dem Vollverb** (aber nach einem Hilfsverb und *to be*) stehen
   - Adverbien der Häufigkeit.
     › She **often** has parties.
     I have **never** seen you before!
     We are **always** at home from 5 p.m.
   - andere Adverbien (besonders Zeitadverbien), die sich auf den ganzen Satz beziehen und nicht zu stark betont werden sollen.
     › I **suddenly** realized who the girl was.
     We **already** knew the answer. (*knew* wird betont)
     We knew the answer **already**. (*already* wird betont)

4. **Adverbien der Art und Weise** stehen
   - unbetont vor dem Vollverb: The population **quickly** doubled.
   - meist nach dem Vollverb: She drives **carefully** in her new car.
   - nach Vollverb + Objekt: He speaks English **excellently**.
   - nach Präposition + Objekt: They looked at the picture **carefully**.

Aufgabe 5

Imagine you are spending a few days in the English countryside. You naturally want to know how you should behave in the country. Read the advice in the *Country Code* and list the adverbs in the categories 1–4 in the rules on page 15.

When you are walking or camping in the country, you should always observe

The Country Code

1. If you are walking in the country: Keep to the paths. You should never walk across fields where crops are growing. Most paths are clearly marked. Follow them carefully and don't take short cuts. Farmers don't usually mind if you walk across a meadow where cows or sheep are grazing. Sometimes there is high grass in a field which a farmer has planted specially. If you thoughtlessly walk across this field, it will be difficult for the farmer to cut the hay later.

2. If you are camping: Always ask permission before you camp in a field. Farmers will not often refuse permission (even though they almost always charge a small sum of money). In dry summers, which we have been having, it is very easy to start a field or forest fire. Don't have a barbecue unless you are perfectly sure that your fire is safe. It is probably best to ask the farmer first.

3. If you have a dog with you: Keep your dog under control at all times. Dogs often run after other animals. A strange dog will certainly frighten farm animals and may possibly injure them. Dozens of sheep and lambs are killed on British farms each year – and many dogs are shot by angry farmers because their owners have not kept them properly under control, especially during the lambing season.

LOOK AFTER BRITAIN'S COUNTRYSIDE –
IT'S THE ONLY ONE WE HAVE!

1. Adverbien bzw. adverbiale Bestimmungen am Satzanfang: …
2. Adverbien bzw. adverbiale Bestimmungen am Satz- oder Satzteilende: …
3. Adverbien vor dem Vollverb (ohne Adverbien der Art und Weise): …
4. Adverbien der Art und Weise: …

Aufgabe 6

Put the parts of these sentences in the right order.

1. at ten o'clock / we / to bed / go / often
2. they / in London / have / lived / always
3. to Spain / next year / we / are / flying / in the autumn
4. his car / was / driving / fast / not / very / he / luckily
5. never / she / in December / has / been / to London
6. I / TV / watch / at the weekends / rarely
7. nearly / yesterday / he / drove / into a wall / his new e-scooter
8. do you / come / often / on Fridays / to the youth club?

Aufgabe 7

Put the words in these sentences in the right order. You will have to decide which of the words should be *adverbs*, and add the "-ly" ending, if necessary.

1. when we arrived at the campsite / it / late / was / terrible
2. we / at this site / had / stayed / often / before / but / so that was no problem
3. our tent / we put up / quick / unbelievable / and / in our sleeping bags / were / afterwards / soon
4. up / later / about an hour / woke / I
5. someone / quiet / I could hear / walking around the campsite
6. loud / my friend Tom was snoring / beside me
7. he / a / sleeper / heavy / is
8. last / perhaps the warden was / making a / check / quick / before going to his own bed / happy
9. I / quiet / heard / very / voices / then
10. soft / were talking / a man and a woman / to each other
11. "impossible / this is / a(n) / place / absolute / !" said the man
12. "here / we / possible / can't / put up our tent / in the middle of the night. People are trying to sleep!"
13. "If we / early / and arrived / had left / before midnight / here / everything would have been OK."
14. "Now we'll have to / get up / and ask the warden / early / if we can stay. It's all your fault."
15. "Why / my fault / always / is it / ?" asked the man. "You're the one / keen / who is / terrible / so / on camping / !"
16. "Be / quiet / !" whispered the woman. "someone up / You'll wake / ."
17. they didn't know / already / that they had / woken me up

Aufgabe 8

Look at the pictures and tell the story. Use the adjective and adverb forms of the words above the pictures. Use both forms if you can make sensible sentences with them! Start like this:

A day in the country
The weather was very ... when we arrived in the Scottish Highlands. The sun was shining ...

1 bright

2 happy

3 careful

4 early

5 lazy

6 sudden

7 quick

8 calm

9 excited

10 unlucky

1.3 Adjektiv oder Adverb?

Um Adjektive und Adverbien richtig verwenden zu können, musst du den Unterschied zwischen beiden Wortarten kennen.
Das **Adjektiv** beschreibt eine Person oder einen Gegenstand, also das Subjekt des Satzes.
Das **Adverb** beschreibt die Handlung, also das Verb näher.

Daher steht nach Verben, die **Zustände** (*to be*) oder **Zustandsänderungen** (*to get, to become*) ausdrücken, die **Adjektivform**, nicht die Adverbform, da das nach dem Verb folgende Wort das Subjekt, nicht das Verb beschreibt.

Adjektiv	Adverb
› **She** was **happy** to see me. **I** got **angry** with him.	› She **smiled** happi**ly**. I began to **shout** angri**ly**.

Auch bei einigen wenigen Verben der **sinnlichen Wahrnehmung** (*look* = aussehen, *taste, smell, sound, feel*) bezieht sich das hinter dem Verb stehende Wort (wie ein Adjektiv) auf das Subjekt.

Adjektiv	Adverb der Art und Weise
› **That food** looks **good**. = **That** food is **good**.	› He **looked carefully** at the food.
This cake tastes **nice**.	If you **ask** me **nicely**, I'll give you some.
The meat smells **bad**.	I can't **smell properly** because I've got a cold.
It is **very cold**. – That's because it's been in the fridge.	He **felt** his way **carefully** through the dark room to the door.
That music sounds **wonderful**.	She **plays** the piano **wonderfully**.

Aufgabe 9

Make sentences from this switchboard, but be careful to use the right form – *adjective* or *adverb*.

1. The CD 2. We 3. She 4. The explorers 5. Jackie 6. My teacher 7. The food 8. The visitors 9. Her singing 10. I	smelt looked felt criticized tasted gave screamed sounded	me their way a	careful/ly unusual/ly angry/angrily terribl(e)/ly delicious/ly beautiful/ly loud/loudly	at the picture. along the tunnel. scream. when he/she saw my homework. after my flight.

Aufgabe 10

A vocabulary exercise to finish off with. Sometimes we combine an adverb and an adjective to make one adjective, like this:

A river which flows fast is a *fast-flowing* river.
A boy who behaves badly is a *badly-behaved* boy.

Do the same with the following definitions.

1. An aircraft which flies high is a ______________________.
2. A person who dresses well is a ______________________.
3. A battery which lasts a long time is a ______________________.
4. A rock concert that has been organized well is a ______________________ ______________________.
5. A lesson which has not been prepared well is a ______________________ ______________________.
6. A rose which smells sweet is a ______________________.
7. A person who looks attractive is an ______________________.
8. A vehicle which moves fast is a ______________________.
9. A display which has been scratched badly is a ______________________.
10. Ground which lies low is ______________________.

Abschlusstest online 1

Herzlichen Glückwunsch! Du hast **Kapitel 1 – Adjektiv und Adverb** durchgearbeitet.
Jetzt weißt du wieder ganz genau, wann du Adjektive und wann du Adverbien verwenden musst und wie diese gesteigert werden. Außerdem kannst du sie an die richtige Stelle im Satz setzen.

So funktioniert der Abschlusstest online:
Um deinen Lernerfolg zu überprüfen, kannst du nun die Tests online machen. Gehe auf
www.klasse5bis10.klett-lerntraining.de/5X7F
und registriere dich wie vorne im Buch beschrieben.

Welche Tests es gibt, siehst du unten in der Tabelle. Nach jedem Test bekommst du eine Auswertung.

Willst du immer im Blick haben, welche Themen du schon kannst oder was du besser nochmal wiederholen solltest? Dann notiere deine Ergebnisse aus den Abschlusstests in der Tabelle.

Mein Ergebnis im Abschlusstest – Kapitel 1

Thema	Mein Ergebnis
Adjektiv und Adverb	

2 Zeitformen zur Wiedergabe von Gegenwart und Zukunft

2.1 Der Gebrauch von *simple present* und *present progressive*

Die beiden Präsens-Zeitformen

Das englische ***simple present*** kann für fast alles benutzt werden – nur nicht für das, was gerade in der Gegenwart abläuft! Hierfür brauchst du die ***progressive form***.
Da es im Deutschen keine Verlaufsformen gibt, werden Extrawörter wie z. B. *zur Zeit, gerade, bin dabei* benutzt, die im Englischen nicht nötig sind und meist auch nicht übersetzt werden.

1. Einfache Beispiele

Deutsch	Englisch	
	Simple form	***Progressive form***
Spricht er Französisch? (allgemein)	**Does** he **speak** French?	
Spricht sie **gerade** Italienisch?		**Is** she **speaking** Italian?
Wir **wohnen** in Deutschland.	We **live** in Germany.	
Sie **wohnt nicht** hier. (allgemeiner Zustand)	She **doesn't live** here.	
Er **kocht gerade**.		He **is cooking**.
Sie **kocht nicht** (mehr).		She **isn't cooking** now.

Deutsch	Englisch	
	Simple form	***Progressive form***
Sie **kommen immer** spät an.	They **always** arrive late.	
Er **macht** seine Haus- aufgaben **oft** im Bus.	He **often does** his homework on the bus.	
Ich **mache gerade** meine Hausaufgaben. (jetzt)		I**'m doing** my homework.

Das ***simple present*** wird für permanente Zustände und regelmäßig wiederholte Tätigkeiten verwendet.
Signalwörter: *always, often, sometimes, never, rarely, seldom, occasionally, every morning* …

Das ***present progressive*** wird für das, was gerade geschieht, verwendet.
Signalwörter: *now, at present, at the moment, just, for the time being* …

2. Kniffligere Beispiele

Deutsch	Englisch	
	Simple form	***Progressive form***
Morgen verlasse ich die Schule. Angabe der Zukunft: Präsens im Deutschen …		**Tomorrow I'm leaving** school. *present progressive* im Englischen!
Er **kommt immer** zu spät an! (… Das ist sehr ärger- lich!)		He**'s always arriving** late! *Always* wird sonst nur mit dem *simple present* benutzt.
Unsere Reise **fängt** am Montag **an**.	Our trip **starts** on Monday.	
Dein Zug **fährt** um sieben.	Your train **leaves** at seven.	

Beide Sätze sind Beispiele der sogenannten „Fahrplanzukunft".

Aufgabe 1

Which form is correct: a), b), c) or d)?

1. John and Alison ______ German at school.
   a) learn   b) are learnt   c) is learning   d) learns
2. John and Alison ______ English, so they can't come out to play.
   a) learn   b) are learnt   c) are learning   d) learns
3. We sometimes ______ to pop concerts.
   a) are going   b) go   c) are gone   d) were going
4. What ______ for! Let's start!
   a) are we waiting   b) we wait   c) do we wait   d) we do wait
5. Are you busy tomorrow? – Yes, I ______ tennis with Roger.
   a) play   b) am playing   c) will play   d) shall play
6. She ______ always ______ that loud disco music! I can't stand it!
   a) is … playing   b) playing   c) play   d) does … play

Aufgabe 2

Translate these sentences into English.

1. Meine Mutter arbeitet zur Zeit nicht in einem Büro.
2. Jan und Marie spielen jede Woche Tennis.
3. Gehst du immer um halb acht in die Schule?
4. Er spielt ständig seine Geige!
5. Jetzt lernen sie Spanisch.
6. Geht sie nie schwimmen?
7. Er hört selten Jazz.
8. Nächste Woche gehe ich in ein Rockkonzert.
9. Der letzte Bus fährt um Mitternacht.

Aufgabe 3

On a sheet of paper list the present tense forms in the advertisement on page 25 under the three headings:

Simple form	Progressive form	Modal auxiliaries
…	…	…

See Britain this year

If you are planning a holiday with a difference, come to England this year!

The south
The Channel coast, from Kent to Dorset, has some of the finest beaches in Britain. The White Cliffs of Dover stand guard over England's biggest ferry port. You can explore the quiet country lanes in your own car. But please drive carefully and watch out for people who want to explore the countryside on foot or on horseback.

The south-west
Devon and Cornwall lie in the extreme south-west of England. Visit Dartmoor and Exmoor, where ponies still live wild. Come to Plymouth and stay at one of the historic old inns that are waiting to welcome you. Are you thinking of spending longer than a week here? Then you might like to rent one of the holiday flats which are to be found in most of the larger towns. Cornwall possesses many interesting relics of Britain's Industrial Revolution and is still the home of china clay mining.

The Midlands
This is the Heart of England: Shakespeare Country. Every year many thousands of people visit the home of the greatest writer in the English language. Tourists love the lovely stone houses which they find in the Cotswolds. Who could resist places which have names like *Bourton-on-the-Water, Stow-on-the-Wold or Moreton-in-Marsh*? But the charm of the Cotswolds does not end with the historic past. Visitors come from all over Europe to explore the beautiful countryside.

The north
Who says there is nothing to see in the North of England?! Not twenty miles from the centre of Manchester lies some of England's prettiest moorland scenery. Yorkshire, with its lovely Dales and its capital, York, where nearly 2,000 years of history are waiting to be discovered. Visit Hadrian's Wall on the old Roman border between England and Scotland. It runs from Carlisle on the west coast to Newcastle on the east and is the biggest single national monument in Britain.

What are you waiting for? Request for our big, free 64-page brochure *Hello England* here. We are looking forward to seeing you in England next year!

Verben, die normalerweise nicht in der Verlaufsform stehen

***to be*, *to have*,** **modale Hilfsverben** (*can*, *must*, *may*, *ought to* …)	**Ausnahme:** Wenn *to be* oder *to have* anstelle eines anderen Verbs benutzt werden, z. B.: He **is being** very difficult. (= behaving badly) We**'re having** breakfast. (= eating) She **is having** a wonderful time. (= enjoying) I**'m having** a bath/shower. (= taking)

Gefühle, Emotionen (in steigender Gefühlsstärke)

like/love/adore:	He **likes**/**loves**/**adores** strawberry ice cream.
dislike/hate/loathe:	She **dislikes**/**hates**/**loathes** parties.
want/wish/desire/need:	I **want**/**wish**/**desire**/**need** to see you.
mind:	**Don't** you **mind** living alone?

Besitzverhältnisse

belong:	This book **belongs** to me.
owe:	She still **owes** me £25.
own/possess:	They **own** three cars at the moment.

Geistige Aktivitäten (wissen, glauben, denken, vergessen etc.)

agree:	He **doesn't agree** with what they are doing.
believe/think:	I **don't think**/**believe** you are listening to me.
forget/remember/ recall/recollect:	She **remembers** her childhood very clearly.
know:	**Do** you **know** what he is talking about?
mean/signify:	What **does** this word **mean**/**signify**?
realize/perceive:	He **realizes** now that he is wrong.
see (= understand):	**Don't** you **see** what I mean?
trust:	I think she **trusts** me now.
understand/appreciate:	I **appreciate** your difficult position.

Einige (aber nicht alle) **Verben der sinnlichen Wahrnehmung**

feel (= *sich **an**fühlen*):	This material **feels** soft and warm.
smell/taste:	The food **smells**/**tastes** good.
sound:	That music **sounds** very familiar. **Ausnahme**: I wonder how she **feels**/**is feeling**? (= ***sich** fühlen*)

Aufgabe 4

Put the verbs in brackets into the right form – *simple* or *progressive*.

1. **(not listen)**	Kevin! You … to me. Wake up!
2. **(go, we – go)**	We usually … to Spain but this year … to England.
3. **(have)**	We had a phone call from some friends. They … a wonderful time there at the moment.
4. **(have)**	They … two young children.
5. **(they – stay)**	Where …? – In Cornwall. It's warm down there.
6. **(have)**	Every morning they … breakfast on the balcony.
7. **(take)**	Then they … a walk along the beach.
8. **(drive)**	On Thursday they … to Land's End.
9. **(they – come)**	When … back? – Next weekend.
10. **(you – know)**	… Sue Hennell?
11. **(not think)**	I … so.
12. **(she – live)**	Where …?
13. **(stay)**	I'm not sure. I think she … with her aunt and uncle for a few weeks.
14. **(you – mean, always arrive)**	… the tall girl with red hair who … late for school?
15. **(believe, be)**	Yes, I … she … often late.
16. **(not see)**	That's why I … her often.
17. **(be, you)**	So why … you so interested in her?
18. **(owe, need)**	She … me £5 and I … the money.

Aufgabe 5

Write an email to an English student. Tell him/her all about yourself. The switchboard will help you. Write at least eight sentences. Start like this:

Don't put words in the same sentence just because they are in the same line.

Dear Rob / Dear Anna, My name is … and I live in …

1. At the moment 2. 3. Sometimes 4. Every week 5. 6. On Saturdays 7. 8. During the week	I my family we	often seldom usually never	(am) (is) (are)	go live learn eat drink …	(…ing)	just now.

2.2 Der Gebrauch des *going to-future* und des *will-future*

going to + Infinitiv

Die Form *going to* + Infinitiv wird für eine zukünftige Handlung benutzt, die beabsichtigt ist. Eine Zeitangabe ist nicht unbedingt erforderlich.

› I'm **going to meet** my friend at the station tomorrow.
He**'s going to** lend me his bicycle.

will-future (*will* + Infinitiv)

Das *will*-Futur wird verwendet

- in *if*-Sätzen.
  › We **won't come** to your party if you aren't nice to us!
  Unless you stop smoking you**'ll** never **lose** your cough.

- als „neutrale" Zukunftsform für Handlungen, die sich ereignen werden.
  › How old **will** Kristin **be** next year? – Fifteen.
  After a dry start, rain **will fall** in some areas.
  The film **will be shown** in the village hall.

- als „spontane Reaktion".
  › The phone's ringing and I'm in the bath! – OK, I**'ll answer** it.
  This exercise is very difficult. – We**'ll help** you.
  What **shall** we **do**? – Don't worry. I**'ll think** of something."

- für Bitten, die als Frage gestellt werden, sowie für Reaktionen darauf.
  › **Will** you **shut** up! – I **won't**! I**'ll shout** and **scream**!
  What **will** you **have**? – I**'ll have** a cup of coffee.

- mit Verben, die normalerweise nicht in der Verlaufsform benutzt werden.
  › I hope you **won't think** I'm being rude.
  When **will** we **know** the results of our test?

- nach Verben, die eine Meinung, Annahme usw. über die Zukunft ausdrücken, wie z. B. *assume, believe, expect, hope, know, think* sowie mit den Adverbien *certainly, perhaps, possibly, probably, surely*.
  › I **hope** you**'ll take** a break after this exercise!
  Do you think she**'ll mind** if we borrow her bike?
  Surely she **won't tell** her friends!

shall oder *will*?

Die Form *shall* wird fast immer nur in Fragen im Sinne von „Soll ich?", „Wollen/Sollen wir?" benutzt. In Aussagesätzen werden beide Formen auf *'ll* abgekürzt.

› Shall I call a taxi? – No, that's OK. I'll walk.
When shall we meet again? – What about next Tuesday?
(= *Wann* ***sollen/wollen*** *wir uns wiedersehen*?)
When will we meet again? – Who knows? Perhaps never.
(= *Wann* ***werden*** *wir uns wohl* ***wiedersehen***?)

Du musst also zwischen der Wettervorhersage (*will*), einer festen Absicht (*going to* + Infinitiv), einer moralischen Pflicht (*shall we*?) und anderen Nuancierungen der Zukunft unterscheiden lernen.

Aufgabe 6

Write two ways of reacting to the same situation.

1. You haven't got much money.
   a) You ask a friend to lend you a few pounds until next week:
   "Will you lend me a few pounds until next week?" (= Bitte)
   b) Your friend agrees but hasn't got much money on him today. He promises to lend you some money tomorrow. The next day he forgets. You remind him:
   "Are you going to lend me that money or not?" (= Absicht)
2. A friend asks you about your trip to London.
   a) Next week? b) Buy me a souvenir? Please!
3. It's a hot day and the window is shut.
   a) You think it would be a good idea to open it – but ask the others first!
   b) Perhaps the traffic noise might be too loud. Ask the others what they think.
4. You go into a sweet shop with a friend. She buys some sweets – but doesn't offer you one! After a while you say:
   a) Not offer me one? b) You – have a stomache ache if you eat them all!
5. It is dark. The doorbell rings, but you know the door is locked and you live on the fourth floor in an old house with no house telephone. Who is going to answer the door?
   a) Nobody moves. At last you stand up and say: "OK, …!"
   b) You ask your brother. "(not – answer the door?)"

Aufgabe 7

How would you react in the following situations? You are walking along the road to school when suddenly you see one car crash into another! What do you think or say?

1. You turn away and walk on. You don't want to get involved.

   You think to yourself:

   "**(I – not get involved)** *I'm not going to get involved.*"

2. As you walk away you look around. The road is empty, so you think to yourself: "**(I – not stop)** ____________________"

3. "**(nobody – see me)** ____________________ if I walk away."

4. You stop and listen. There is no sound. No people on the road – no traffic. You think: "**(someone – arrive – in a few minutes)**

   ____________________."

   (be late for school) ____________________ if I wait any longer!"

5. But you can't walk any further. Perhaps the people are injured. You walk back to the cars. One driver is sitting beside his car with his head in his hands. You ask him: "**(I – call an ambulance?)** ____________________

   ____________________."

6. The injured man doesn't say anything at first. You say: "Don't move!

   (I – call an ambulance!) ____________________"

7. He looks up and says: "OK, **(I – not move)** ____________________"

8. You look at the other car. There is a young woman in it. She is unconscious. You say: "I hope **(she – OK)** ____________________"

9. The injured man says: "**(try and get her out?)** ____________________"

10. You can't open the door on the driver's side. You think it may be best if you do not move the woman: "____________________"

11. The injured man asks you to call the police too: "____________________"

12. You say: "Yes, OK, it ____________________ **(not long)**!"

2.4 Das future progressive

Es gibt auch eine Verlaufsform des ***will-future***. Wie bei allen Verlaufsformen drückt *will be …-ing* eher eine längere Handlung als eine Punkthandlung aus.

Verben, die kurze „Einmalhandlungen" ausdrücken, stehen natürlich immer im einfachen ***will-future***, wie z. B. *ask*, *stop*, *start*, *see*, *buy*.

Die Verlaufsform der Zukunft bietet sich also speziell für Verben an, die **nicht** Kurzhandlungen beschreiben, wie z. B. *live*, *work*, *sit*, *lie*, *wait*, *listen*, *watch*, *stay*, usw.

Vergleiche:

Will-future	***Future progressive***
Next year we **will move** to the USA.	Next year we **will be living** in the USA.
We**'ll stay** at a nice hotel. (*ein Versprechen*)	We**'ll stay** at a nice hotel.
I **won't wait** for her much longer! (*mein Entschluss*)	I **won't be waiting** outside the cinema. (*ich werde woanders warten*)
Come and see me tomorrow and I**'ll bake** a cake. (= I'll bake it before you come.)	Don't come before two o'clock. I**'ll be baking** a cake. (= I'll be busy doing something else if you come too early.)
Our train **will arrive** at five o'clock. Don't be late! (= The train is never late – always on time.)	Our train **will be arriving** at about five o'clock. (= You're not sure about the exact time, or perhaps the train is usually late!)

Aufgabe 8

Say what the people will be doing at two o'clock this afternoon.

1 Sue – travel

2 John – iron

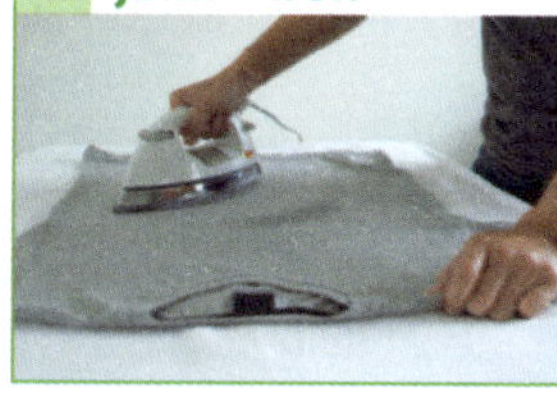

3 Mrs Baker

4 Mr Baker – garden

5 Julia

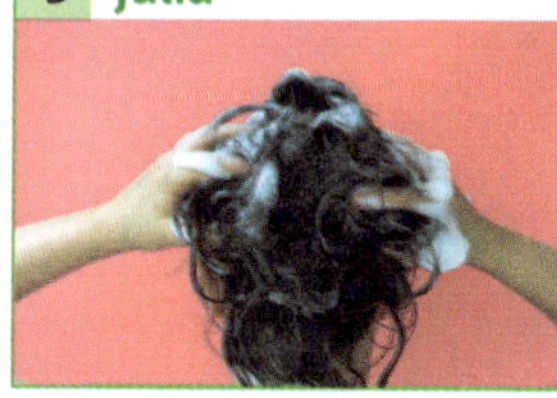

6 the girls

7 our teacher

8 Chloe and Anna

9 our cat – have lunch

Aufgabe 9

Put the right halves of the sentences together.

1. What will you do
2. What will you be doing
3. Don't hit him or
4. Don't disturb him because
5. Will they be having lunch
6. Will they have lunch
7. If we arrive late
8. When we arrive
9. She'll finish work
10. She'll be finishing work

a) at exactly ten past five.
b) he'll probably be sleeping.
c) we will all have breakfast.
d) about now.
e) this time next week?
f) before we arrive?
g) he'll tell the police!
h) if you can't find the key?
i) they will be having breakfast.
j) when we arrive?

2.3 Das *future perfect*

Das ***future perfect*** wird für Handlungen verwendet, die in der **Zukunft abgeschlossen werden**.

› Next year I **will try** to learn Spanish.
In two years' time I **will have learnt** a lot of Spanish
because I **will have been learning** it for two years.

Wie immer drückt die einfache Form dieser ***future perfect tense*** eine Punkthandlung bzw. einen Punktzustand aus – hier den erreichten Stand des Wissens –, während die ***progressive form*** den andauernden Spracherwerb betont.

› Mr Wells **is retiring** next month.
How long **will** he **have been** a teacher at your school?
He **will have been teaching** English there for 45 years.
He **will have taught** three generations of students!

Es gibt auch einen Unterschied zwischen diesen beiden Sätzen:

1. **Will** you **finish** reading your book when we get back?	Das ist eine Bitte: Lies dein Buch zu Ende, wenn wir wieder zu Hause sind.
2. **Will** you **have finished** reading your book when we get back?	Das ist die Frage, ob du es wohl bis dahin fertig gelesen haben wirst.

Aufgabe 10

This is what you are doing now. But how much will you have done in the future? Be careful – sometimes you will need the *progressive form*!

1. I am learning to ride an e-scooter now, but when I am 19 ______________ ______________________ **(pass my driving test)**.
2. Rosie is training to be a bank clerk. In two years' time ______________ ______________ **(finish her training)**.
3. We are moving to Bristol next month. When we leave our present house ______________________ **(live there for 10 years)**.

→

4. How long ______________________ **(you learn English)** when you leave school?
5. Where's Mike? He's talking to Sally on the phone. How long has he been talking to her? In five minutes he ______________________ **(talk)** to her for exactly an hour!
6. I expect John is waiting at the station already. Never mind. We'll be there in half an hour. He ______________________ **(not wait)** long!
7. This time next week our English teacher ______________________ **(mark)** our tests.
8. I'm saving £10 a week. I'm 16 now, so when I'm 18 I ______________________ **(save)** for two years.
9. I hope I ______________________ **(save)** enough to pay for my driving lessons.
10. ______________________ **(they – arrive)** at the airport yet? – I expect so.
11. In 2027 my mum ______________________ **(work)** at the same office for 25 years.
12. Really? My mum ______________________ **(finish)** working by then.
13. Shall we take the new motorway to Edinburgh when we go on holiday this summer? I don't think ______________________ **(they finish)** building it by then.
14. Tarik's a permanent student. Next term he ______________________ **(study English)** at university for seven years!
15. If we don't hurry up they ______________________ **(drink)** all the wine before we even arrive at the party!

Abschlusstest online 2

Großartig! Du hast **Kapitel 2 – Zeitformen zur Wiedergabe von Gegenwart und Zukunft** durchgearbeitet. Hier hast du einige Tricks kennengelernt, die dir helfen, dich für die richtige Präsensform zu entscheiden, *going to*- und *will-future* kannst du sicher anwenden und die verschiedenen Verlaufsformen von Präsens und Futur sind keine Fremdworte für dich.

So funktioniert der Abschlusstest online:
Um deinen Lernerfolg zu überprüfen, kannst du nun die Tests online machen. Gehe auf
www.klasse5bis10.klett-lerntraining.de/5X7F
und registriere dich wie vorne im Buch beschrieben.

Welche Tests es gibt, siehst du unten in der Tabelle. Nach jedem Test bekommst du eine Auswertung.

Willst du immer im Blick haben, welche Themen du schon kannst oder was du besser nochmal wiederholen solltest? Dann notiere deine Ergebnisse aus den Abschlusstests in der Tabelle.

Mein Ergebnis im Abschlusstest – Kapitel 2

Thema	Mein Ergebnis
Die Zeitformen der Gegenwart	
Die Zeitformen der Zukunft	

3 Zeitformen der Vergangenheit

3.1 Das *past tense: Simple* oder *progressive form*?

Die ***simple form*** drückt eine oder mehrere Handlungen aus, die in einem abgeschlossenen Zeitraum in der Vergangenheit passierte(n).

› We **visited** London last year.
We **visited** London several times last year.

1. Als Kontrast zu einer in der ***simple form*** stehenden, relativ wichtigen Handlung wird die ***progressive form*** oft für eine „Hintergrundhandlung" benutzt.
   › We **visited** London several times while we **were staying** in Brighton.

2. Das ***past progressive*** steht selten allein. In solchen Fällen schildert es entweder nur den Hintergrund oder eine langsame Entwicklung (= Verlauf).
   › I looked out of the window. It **was** still **raining**.
   It **was getting** light. The birds **were beginning** to sing.

   Vergleiche dazu:
   › As soon as it **got** light, the birds **began** to sing.

   Relativ schneller Sonnenaufgang (wie in den Tropen) – plötzlich einsetzender Vogelgesang. Hier könnte auch eine immer wiederkehrende Alltagssituation gemeint sein.

3. Manchmal wird die Gleichzeitigkeit von zwei Handlungen dadurch betont, dass beide in der Verlaufsform stehen. Die Frage erkundigt sich nach dem Verlauf bereits begonnener Handlungen.
   › What **were** they **doing** when you arrived?
   John **was cooking** and Susie **was cutting** the grass.

   Die Frage müsstest du aber anders stellen, wenn du die Reaktion auf die Ankunft des Gastes beschreiben wolltest.
   › What **did** they **do** when you arrived?
   John **cooked** lunch and Susie **cut** the grass.
   Die Antwort betont nicht den gleichzeitigen Verlauf, sondern nur die Tatsache, dass beide Handlungen relativ gleichzeitig anfingen und zu Ende gingen.

4. *was …-ing* (oft mit *going to*-Futur) hat häufig die Bedeutung „wollte", „hatte vor". Das Hilfsverb muss stark betont werden.
   › She ***was* meeting** Patrick this evening, but she has changed her mind.
   They ***were* going to call** the fire brigade, but they managed to put the fire out themselves.

Merke:
Viele Verben können sowohl in der ***simple*** als auch in der ***progressive form*** verwendet werden.
Die Voraussetzung für die Verwendung eines Verbs in der Verlaufsform ist allerdings, dass es eine Handlung ausdrückt, die von einer gewissen Dauer sein muss.
Kurze Handlungen (*to start, to finish, to drop, to see, to hear* usw.) sowie Zustände, Gefühle und sonstige „Nichthandlungen" (z.B. *to have, to own, to contain, to owe, to like, to feel, to want* usw.) werden **fast nie** in der ***progressive form*** ausgedrückt.

Tipp: Eine nützliche Aufzählung solcher Verben findest du auf S. 26.

Love Story?

A light rain was falling when I reached the station. I was going home after my first term at university, and I was feeling very happy. At the time I was studying in Edinburgh and my parents were living in London. I was very much looking forward to going home because my girlfriend Rosie would be meeting me at Kings Cross Station. It was December – almost Christmas. Many of my friends were travelling south on the same train, and there were a lot of well-known – and even more half-known – faces on the platform at Edinburgh's Waverley Station that morning as we waited for the Flying Scotsman. The train would be very crowded.

It was while I was looking for a seat that I saw her. My heart stopped. The girl of my dreams was sitting there reading a paperback novel, and opposite her was one of the few empty seats on the train. The train was still standing at the platform. Other young people were putting their bags and suitcases between the seats or on the luggage racks. Nobody seemed to have seen the empty seat – or the girl – except me. "Is this seat taken?" I heard myself ask. I couldn't believe it was actually me speaking. She looked up, smiled and said, "No, I was keeping this seat free for my boyfriend, but he hasn't arrived yet." I sat down opposite her, wondering what to say next. Just then the train began to move. I watched the platform slide backwards as the train gathered speed, and as I was watching I suddenly saw a young man with a heavy suitcase. He was running after the train. Was this her delayed boyfriend? Only I could see him. She was facing the other way. But the train was travelling quite fast now, so he couldn't catch it.

Before five minutes had passed Alicia (that was her name) and I were talking as if we had known each other for years. In those days it took five hours to travel from Edinburgh to London, even on a train like the Flying Scotsman, which only stopped at Newcastle. By the time we were passing through York I knew that I had found myself a new girlfriend.

Alicia didn't actually live in London, but she was staying with an uncle and aunt over Christmas. We exchanged addresses and telephone numbers and promised each other that we would meet at a pub for a few drinks at the earliest opportunity. I had forgotten Rosie.

We were ten minutes late at Kings Cross. I helped Alicia off the train with her luggage. She smiled and suddenly put her arms around my neck to kiss me goodbye. I looked up from the kiss and saw that Rosie was walking quickly along the platform towards us.

She was not smiling.

Aufgabe 1

Read the story on page 38 and list the parts of the text that contain a contrasting form in the past. Look at the example.

Simple form	Progressive form
	A light rain was falling
when I reached the station.	
I read the magazine	*while I was waiting.*

Aufgabe 2

Make a list of the past progressive forms in the text and put them in the following categories.

Background description	*was ...-ing = wollte*
...	...

Aufgabe 3

Put the two halves of the sentences together.

1. She was talking to me when	a) they met at the pub.
2. Before the robber entered the bank,	b) the girls were watching TV.
3. When we went on holiday,	c) she was wearing a mask.
4. John talked to Susie when	d) all our clothes were stolen.
5. First they bought the tickets, then	e) the train arrived.
6. While we were playing tennis,	f) the dog stole the sausages.
7. The boys grilled the meat while	g) the phone rang.
8. When I last saw the bank robber,	h) they got on the train.
9. They were on the platform when	i) we always locked all the doors.
10. The boys were grilling the meat when	j) she put a mask on.

Du hast sicher schon erkannt, dass *while* (= während) logischerweise mit der *progressive form* und *when* (= als) mit der *simple form* verwendet wird. Es gibt Ausnahmen, aber du kannst dich normalerweise auf diese Faustregel verlassen.

Aufgabe 4

Use the verbs below to complete the following sentences. Each verb should be used twice: once in the simple form and once in the *progressive form*.

say talk wait do have see

1. We ______________________ twenty-five minutes for a Number 68 bus yesterday.
2. While we ______________________, three Number 196 buses came.
3. What ________ you ________ to the conductor when the bus arrived?
4. Nothing. Sue ______________________ to me non-stop.
5. I couldn't hear what anybody else ______________________.
6. I ________________ Sue in town yesterday. She wasn't at school.
7. Have you any idea what she ______________________ there?
8. She wants to leave school this summer. She ______________________ someone about a job in a bank.
9. She ______________________ to the bank manager for over an hour.
10. What ________ she ________ after her interview?
11. She ______________________ a cup of coffee at a café.
12. That's right. When I saw her she ______________________ a cup of coffee.

Aufgabe 5

Tell the story. Write one sentence for each picture. Use one simple form and one progressive form for each picture and start each sentence with the words in picture, like this:

1. While I was walking to school one morning, I saw an accident.

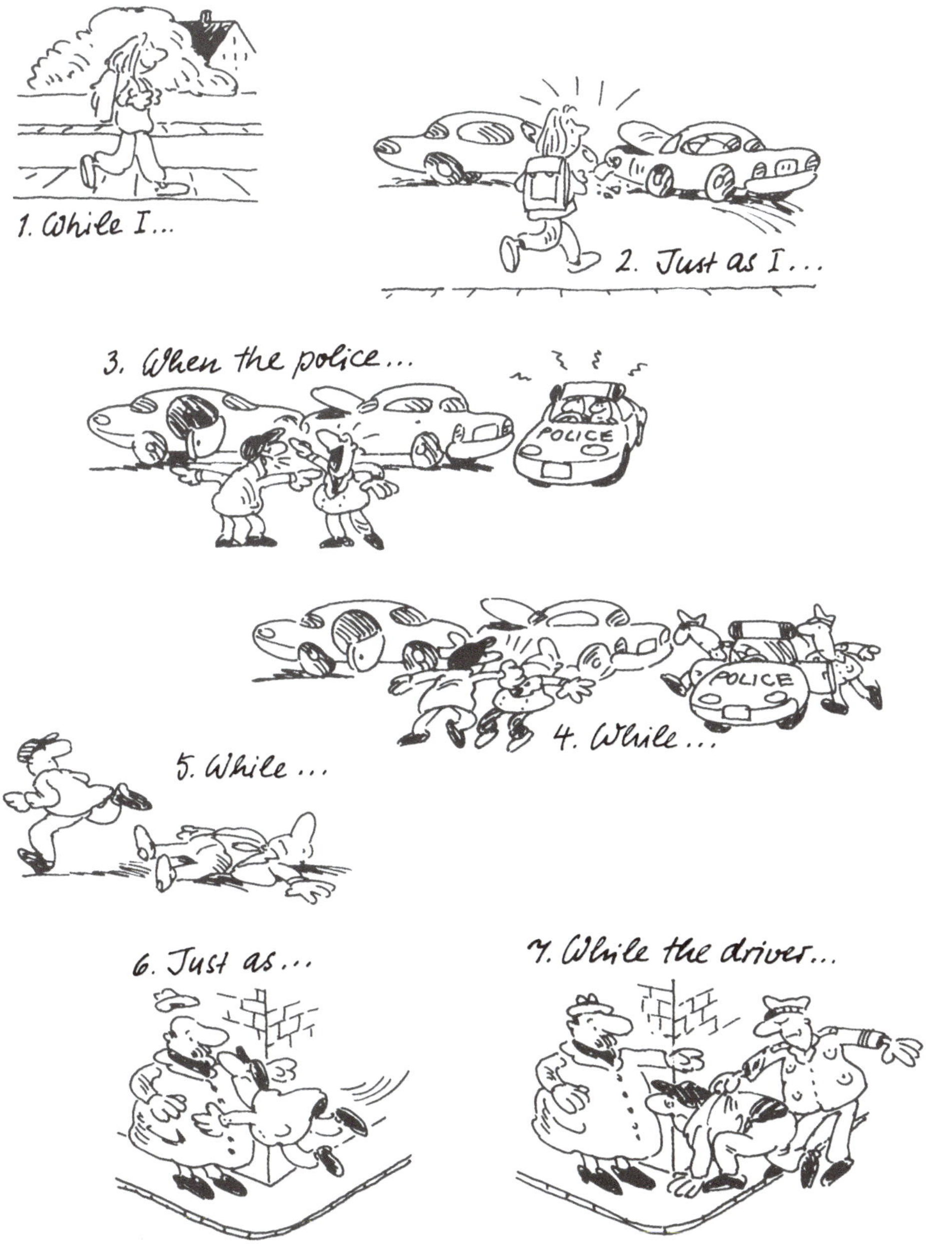

3.2 *Present perfect* oder *simple past*?

simple past

Das ***simple past*** wird verwendet,

- wenn ein Zeitraum in der Vergangenheit erwähnt wird.
  › We **went** there last week.
  Where **were** you last night?
- wenn der Zeitpunkt in der Vergangenheit wichtiger ist als die Tatsache selbst.
  › When **did** they **arrive**? – At six o'clock.
- wenn mehrere Handlungen in der Vergangenheit (z.B. in einer Geschichte) aufeinander folgen.
  › I **woke** up, **washed**, **dressed** and **had** breakfast before I **left** for school.

present perfect

Das ***present perfect*** wird verwendet,

- wenn ein Zeitraum in der Vergangenheit nicht erwähnt wird.
  › We **have been** there.
  Where **have** you **been**?
- wenn eine Handlung nicht in der Vergangenheit, sondern in der Gegenwart endet.
  › They**'ve** just **arrived**.
  I**'ve finished** my work.
- wenn eine in der Vergangenheit begonnene Handlung in die Gegenwart und vermutlich darüber hinaus weitergeführt wird.
  › We**'ve** always **lived** here.

Darüber hinaus verwendest du das *present perfect*

- für Handlungen, die in der Gegenwart zu Ende gehen.
  Signalwörter: *now*, (*only*) *just* …
  › The rain **has** just **stopped**.
- für abgeschlossene Handlungen, die sich in der Vergangenheit ereigneten, aber keine Zeitangabe enthalten.
  Signalwörter: *often*, *several times* …
  › We **have** often **had** a meal in that snack bar.
- für Ereignisse, die noch nicht passiert sind (*not … yet*), aber noch passieren könnten.
  Signalwörter: *ever*, *not … yet*
  › Have you **ever** been to Spain?
  She has**n't** visited the museum **yet**.

Beachte:
Das ***simple past*** wählst du also nicht nach dem Kriterium „abgeschlossene Handlung", sondern nur für Handlungen in abgeschlossenen Zeiträumen der Vergangenheit, auch wenn diese Zeiträume einem Menschenleben oder einem Abschnitt der Geschichte gleichkommen.

Vergleiche:

She never **visited** Yugoslavia.	She **hasn't visited** Serbia yet.
(*Das Land existiert nicht mehr.*)	(*Das ist noch nicht passiert.*)

Confrontations between police and Asian youths provoked widespread shock.

Over the past years Asians in Britain, particularly Muslims, have felt very worried about the way in which the wider culture of drugs, small crime, prostitution and the exploitation of women has invaded the areas where they live.
Drug-taking has increased within the Asian community, and there have been many cases of crimes connected with the drug-taking habit. A sex magazine with photos of Asian girls has been in circulation for over a year, and a gay magazine for Asians has just appeared and is selling well.
All this undermines the traditional values and family life of the Muslim community, and has generated a climate of moral panic.
Because the family is vital to the success of the Asian middle class, the moral threat to the family is also an economic threat.
Many Asians living in city centres have found that the value of their houses goes down when the area becomes known as a centre for drugs and prostitution.
Muslims have started a campaign to protect themselves against these negative features of the outside culture. The campaign began in Birmingham last year. When repeated complaints to the police and local authorities produced no results, Asians set up vigilante groups to clean up the areas.
This has led to a conflict of values and ways of life.
This conflict need not lead to violence, but often does.
Unemployment is high among Asian young people. Many of them have left school without adequate qualifications, job prospects are poor, and there is still much discrimination in all areas of life.
Young Asians have taken over the moral and religious campaign of the older generation and made it more militant. But they are also more liberal than their parents: they have adopted Western values such as the equality of the sexes, greater freedom of choice where marriage and jobs are concerned, and are thus not only often in conflict with "Western" society but also with the older members of the Asian community. The violent confrontation with police last weekend showed that the older generation of Asians is no longer in control of Asian youth in Britain.

Aufgabe 6

Read the text and list all the forms of the *simple past* and *present perfect* under the following heading.

1. Simple past – completed period of time is given or is clear from the context
2. Present perfect – action still going on
3. Present perfect – action (or actions) completed at an undefined time in the past
4. Present perfect – action takes place in the present or very close to the present

Aufgabe 7

Make ten sensible sentences. Use the verbs below. Look out for any keywords which influence the choice of tense (yesterday, not . . . yet, etc.). Make at least two questions and two negative sentences for each tense.

play visit eat listen to drink watch

Examples: *Have you ever eaten fish and chips?*
I watched a horror film last night.

Have you Did you I We I have We have I / We didn't	ever never often . . .	. . .	the radio yesterday evening "hide and seek" as a child/children beer when I / we / you was / were younger a horror film last night football London last year fish and chips Frankfurt yet concerts on the radio marmalade when I / we / you were in England

Aufgabe 8

Here are some pairs of similar sentences. Each sentence contains one good reason for the choice of tense.
Don't forget: choose the *simple past* for actions in completed periods of time in the past, not just for completed actions. Use the *present perfect* in all cases where the time in the past is not stated or implied.

1. **(go)** Where's Nick? – He ______________ to school.
   Where's Mia? – She ______________ to school ten minutes ago.
2. **(live)** I ______________ here all my life.
   Goethe ______________ there for many years.
3. **(do)** _____ you ______________ your English homework last night?
   _____ you ______________ your English homework yet?
4. **(drive)** We _____ not ______________ to Brighton at the weekend.
   We _____ not ______________ to Brighton since last year.
5. **(learn)** My sister ______________ to drive last year.
   I _____ not ______________ to drive yet.
6. **(write)** Shakespeare ______________ a lot of plays.
   The young author ______________ three plays already.
7. **(buy)** Look! Our neighbours ______________ a new car!
   – Oh! Our neighbours ______________ two new bicycles on Monday. They haven't got a car.
8. **(drink)** _____ you often ______________ coke? – No, not often.
   _____ you often ______________ coke when you lived in France? – Yes.
9. **(fly)** _____ Julie ever ______________ to America? – Not yet.
   When _____ she ______________ to Australia? – In 2018.
10. **(see)** _____ you ______________ Patrick this morning? (at 11.55)
   _____ you ______________ Patrick this morning? (at 12.05)

*zu 4. Die Angabe **since last year** bezieht sich auf einen Zeitabschnitt, der im vorigen Jahr anfängt, jedoch bis in die Gegenwart andauert, also **present perfect**.*

*zu 5. **Last year** bezieht sich hier auf das ganze Jahr als abgeschlossene Zeitspanne, also **simple past**.*

zu 10. Die Frage wird auch um fünf vor zwölf (wo Patrick noch auftauchen könnte) anders gestellt als um fünf nach zwölf, wo der Vormittag bereits vorbei ist.

Beachte:
Die falsche Verwendung der Zeitformen im Englischen rührt oft daher, dass du versuchst, eine Zeitform, die in deiner Muttersprache richtig eingesetzt wird, auch im Englischen zu benutzen.

› Ich **wohne** in Berlin. = I **live** in Berlin.
Ich **wohne** seit fünf Jahren in Berlin. = I **have lived** in Berlin for five years.

Im Deutschen wird richtigerweise die „einfache Gegenwart" in beiden Sätzen verwendet. Aber im Deutschen stellt diese Zeitform nur den Bezug zur Gegenwart (= dauert noch an) her. Die deutsche Perfektform („Ich habe … gelebt …") kann hier nicht – wie im Englischen – für Handlungen verwendet werden, die in der Vergangenheit anfangen und bis in die Gegenwart andauern.

Aufgabe 9

Translate the following sentences into English. Don't translate word for word. Think about the correct tense.

Beachte bei der Übersetzung die Hinweise im Kasten oben.

1. Wir haben diesen Film zweimal gesehen.
2. Wir haben diesen Film letzte Woche gesehen.
3. Er wohnte in Berlin, als ich ihn kannte.
4. Meine Tante arbeitet in einem Büro.
5. Mein Onkel arbeitet seit 2015 in Spanien.
6. Unser Lehrer hat England dreimal besucht.
7. Er wohnt hier seit vier Jahren.
8. Er hat hier ein Jahr gewohnt, bevor er in die USA ging.
9. Sie ist gerade angekommen.
10. Sie kommt immer pünktlich an.

Wenn du diese zehn Sätze alle richtig hast, kann man dir nur gratulieren! Du hast das Problem gepackt! Es bleiben nur ein paar Punkte zu beachten, die mit dem Einsatz des *present perfect* zusammenhängen. Der heikelste Punkt ist wohl die Unterscheidung *for* und *since* (siehe Kapitel 3.3).

Aufgabe 10

Someone has scratched out some words on the notice board. Put them back in.

The Tower of London

The oldest part of the Tower of London, the White Tower, ________ built by William the Conqueror after he became King of England in 1066. The 27-metre-high walls are almost 5 metres thick at the bottom and 3.5 metres thick at the top.

During its long history the Tower ________ used as a palace, a prison and a garrison. It has been enlarged many times. Many people ________ imprisoned or executed here, including Anne Boleyn, second wife of Henry VIII, who ________ beheaded here in 1536. Her ghost and many others ________ seen in various parts of the Tower.

Aufgabe 11

Complete this text by putting the verbs in brackets into the right tense. But be careful! Sometimes the verb should be in the passive.

1. London **(have)** ________ always ________ a traffic problem.
2. In the 1850s it **(be)** ________ already the biggest city in the world and it **(be)** ________ difficult to get quickly from one side of the city to the other.
3. In those days many people **(work)** ________ in the City, London's financial and commercial centre, which is in the east of London, but they **(not live)** ________________ near their offices: they **(prefer)** ________________ to live in the healthy suburbs to the west of London.
4. The first underground railway in the world **(build)** ________________ in 1863.

5. It **(call)** ____________________ the Metropolitan Railway, and many underground railways all over the world **(take over)** ____________________ the name "Metro" from the first Underground.

6. The railway **(run)** ____________________ from Paddington Station in what **(be)** ____________________ then West London, to Farringdon Street in the City of London.

Aufgabe 12

Jenny and Paul want to go camping for the weekend. Jenny is nearly ready now, but she phones Paul to ask if he has done everything. Look at the pictures and continue a dialogue.

Have you checked your bike?

Of course! I checked it last night. Have you packed your tent?

last night
yesterday
this afternoon
just

check bike?

pack tent?

buy food?

pack rucksack?

phone campside?

3.3 Das *present perfect*: *simple* oder *progressive form*?

Present perfect simple und *present perfect progressive* im Vergleich

Das ***present perfect progressive*** wird nur bei **Verben** eingesetzt, die einen **zeitlichen Verlauf darstellen** (*live*, *work*, *wait*, *play*, *watch TV* usw.).

› We **have been living** here since 2015.

Das ***present perfect progressive*** wird **nicht** bei Verben eingesetzt, die nur kurze Handlungen beschreiben (*finish*, *stop*, *decide*, *want* usw.) und deshalb fast immer in der *simple form* verwendet werden.
Vergleiche:

› There you are! I**'ve finished** my homework at last.
I**'ve been working** at it all afternoon!

Bei Verben, die sowohl in der Verlaufsform als auch in der einfachen Form benutzt werden können, betont die Verlaufsform die Dauer einer Handlung, während die einfache Form die Tatsache selbst oder das Ergebnis betont.

› She **has been working** in the garden all day.
She **has worked** very hard. Just look at the garden!

Da Verben in der *progressive form* einen Handlungsverlauf beschreiben, ist in solchen Sätzen oft die Dauer (*all day*, *all my life*, *for ten years*) bzw. der Ausgangspunkt (*since 2021* usw.) angegeben.

Aufgabe 13

Give the reasons why. You will need the *present perfect progressive* form in all your sentences.

1. I'm sorry my hands are dirty but *I've been repairing* (repair/car)
2. You look hot! – Yes, that's because ______________________ (play/football)
3. She doesn't speak much English even though ______________________ (live in London/three years already)
4. How long ______________? (you/wait/here) – About an hour.
5. My bottle of water is almost empty. I think ______________________! (someone/drink/it)

6. Let's stop. We ____________________ (practise/English grammar/3 o'clock)

7. What ____________________? (she/do/all afternoon) – Playing tennis.

8. I'm sorry, but I can't go to the cinema tonight. – Oh! I'm so disappointed!

____________________! (look forward to it/all week)

9. ____________________? (the baby/behave/well) – Oh, yes. So far, at least.

Aufgabe 14

Put the most likely form of the verb in brackets (*present perfect simple* or *progressive*) into the following sentences.

1. **(learn)** ________ you ____________ ten new words today?
2. **(learn)** How long ________ you ____________ English? – Four years.
3. **(see)** I ________n't ____________ John since last week.
4. **(see)** John ____________ Stephanie a lot recently.
   They're very good friends.
5. **(have)** They ____________ lunch for over an hour already.
6. **(have)** They ________ never ____________ real English food.
7. **(work)** She hasn't had much free time recently because she
   ____________ on her school geography project.
8. **(work)** What a wonderful exam result! You ____________ very hard!
9. **(do)** What ________ you ____________ all afternoon? –
   (listen) I ____________ to my CDs.
10. **(do)** The pen I lent you doesn't work now! What ________ you
    ____________ to it?
11. **(play)** You look tired. ________ you ____________ too many
    computer games again?
12. **(be)** ________ you ever ____________ to Gobowen? – Where is
    Gobowen?

Der Gebrauch von *for, since* und *ago*

For und *since* sind besonders häufige Signalwörter für das ***present perfect progressive***. Beide werden im Deutschen mit „seit" übersetzt.
Sie sind aber sowohl voneinander als auch von der deutschen Präposition „vor ... Jahren/Tagen" zu unterscheiden, das im Englischen mit ... *years/days ago* übersetzt wird.

seit = ***since*** + Zeit**punkt**:	I've known her **since** 2010/last week.
seit = ***for*** + Zeit**spanne**:	I've known her **for** three weeks/a few days.
vor = Zeit**punkt** + ***ago***:	She lived here three years **ago**.

Da *ago* immer einen Zeitpunkt in der Vergangenheit markiert, steht das Verb fast immer im ***simple past***.

› I **met** her three days **ago**.

Eine scheinbare Ausnahme bildet die Kombination von ***since*** (*two years*) ***ago***, die eine Zeit**spanne** bezeichnet.

› I've known her **for** three weeks.	(Zeitspanne)
I've known her **since** last month.	(Zeitpunkt)
I've known her **since three weeks ago**.	(Zeitspanne = seit vor drei Wochen)

Da *since* den Anfangszeitpunkt einer Handlung markiert, die bis in die Gegenwart hineinreicht, steht das Verb davor immer im ***present perfect***.
Since wird mit dem ***simple past*** nur in Nebensätzen benutzt, in denen das Verb den Anfangszeitpunkt der Handlung beschreibt. Ein Verb im Nebensatz nach *since* steht also immer im ***simple past***.

› She came to London in February.
I**'ve known** her **since February**.
I**'ve known** her **since** she **came** to London. (= since February)

Aufgabe 15

Make ten sentences from the switchboard using *for*, *since*, *ago* and *since … ago*. Use each construction at least twice.

1. John	have	been learning		… last June.
2. We	has	lived		… three years …
3. She		been working	here	… six weeks.
4. They	came		English	… three months …
5. Peter and Sophia	lived			… they left Berlin.
				…

Aufgabe 16

Complete the following sentences with *for*, *since*, *from*, *ago*.

1. _______ years Christine Meadows wanted to work on the railway.
2. Her wish came true six months _______ .
3. Christine has now been working at Gobowen station _______ last September, _______ she became a sixth-former, in fact.
4. Railways are in the family. Christine's uncle worked as an engine-driver _______ 1985 until he retired in 2015.
5. _______ his retirement, Joe Meadows has been working as part-time stationmaster on a private tourist railway in North Wales.
6. _______ six hours a day during the summer season he sells tickets at the station.
7. Joe works _______ 10 a.m. to 5 p.m. with an hour for lunch.
8. The railway, which was built over 150 years _______ , once transported slate* from the mountains to the sea.
9. But _______ the 1950s it has been a big tourist attraction, and now it only transports passengers.
10. No slate has been transported on it _______ sixty years ago.

* *Schiefer*

Aufgabe 17

Look at the pictures and write a local TV news report about the young men who want to take over the bus service to a small Scottish village. Use a form of the *present perfect* in all the sentences.

1 Last week the Highland Bus Company decided to close down the bus service from Aviemore to the remote Highland village of Strathdon, even though this service … fifty years.

2 The people of Strathdon are very angry. They say …

One woman says …

3 Our reporter Samantha Bevis is in Strathdon tonight. She is talking to some of the villagers. "…?" – "Yes, …"

4 "What are you going to do?" – "Well, we …

5 We'll run the service ourselves. I'm a bus-driver. I …" – "Yes. I think I'm a good driver because …

6 and …"

7 "The villagers of Strathdon …

8 A representative of the bus company … I'll try and have a few words with him after the meeting."

9 "Has the meeting been a success?" – "Well, not really. We … but no real progress …

10 If the young men of the village want to run the bus service we think they should have a try. The bus company …"

Aufgabe 18

Put yourself in the following situations. How would you react?

Situation	Reaction
1. You see a friend who has shaved his/her head. He/she is completely bald! You say: *"What have you done to your hair?"*	do?
2. You can't find your school bag. You think your mother might know where it is.	see?
3. You bought yourself a bar of chocolate yesterday. Today there is only half of it left. You ask your brothers, sisters or friends.	eat?
4. Even worse! All the chocolate is gone – only the wrapper is left!	who/eat?
5. You haven't seen Dave Smith for some time. Perhaps he doesn't live in your town any more. You ask a school friend.	see/recently?
6. You are late for a date with your boyfriend/girlfriend. You run all the way to the cinema, but he/she is already there.	wait/long?
7. There was an article in the newspaper about the oldest man (97) in your town, but you didn't read it. You ask a friend about him.	how long/live here?
8. You are having a party, but your best friend arrives an hour late!	where/be?
9. Someone says "I'm very sorry" to you, but you don't know why.	what/do?
10. Someone arrives at school with very dirty hands.	what/do?
11. You look very tired after this exercise. A friend asks you:	how long/practise/English?

3.4 Das *past perfect*

Simple past und *past perfect* im Satzgefüge

Das ***past perfect*** sorgt für Klarheit in der Handlungsreihenfolge in der Vergangenheit.

› He **rang** the doorbell because he **had forgotten** his key.
  She **got** up, **walked** to the window and **looked** out. It **had snowed** in the night.

Vergleiche die Reihenfolge:

a) When we **arrived**, John **made** lunch.
   1 2

b) When we **arrived**, John **had made** lunch.
   2 1

In Satz a) wird die zeitliche Reihenfolge und die unmittelbare Nähe der Handlungen durch die Verwendung derselben Zeitform festgehalten.
In Satz b) hatte John das Mittagessen bereits gemacht, bevor wir ankamen. Die Reihenfolge im Satz ist umgekehrt, aber die Verwendung des ***past perfect*** schließt Missverständnisse aus.

Die beiden Satzteile in Satz a) können aber auch vertauscht werden, ohne dass ein Missverständnis entsteht.

› John **made** lunch when we **arrived**.

Im Satz „John **made** lunch **after** we **had arrived**." nimmt man an, dass eine längere Pause und eventuell auch andere, nicht erwähnte Aktivitäten dazwischenkamen.

Das ***past perfect*** wird auch nach *when* im Sinne von *after* benutzt.

› **When** he **had told** me his story, he **asked** me to lend him some money.
  (eine Handlung vor der nächsten beendet: *when* = nachdem)

  When he **told** me his story, I **was** shocked.
  (ich war evtl. auch während des Erzählens bereits schockiert: *when* = als, während)

  When I **saw** Derek last week, he **had shaved** his beard off.
  (er hatte seinen Bart bereits abrasiert: *when* = als)

Auch *until* (= erst als, bis) wird mit dem ***past perfect*** benutzt.

› Mum didn't let me watch TV **until** I **had finished** my homework.

Signalwörter für ***past perfect***: *after*, *when* (= *after*), *until* (= erst als)

Aufgabe 19

Use *after* to join the two halves of the sentences.

1. Susie did her homework. Then she took her dog for a walk.
   After Susie had done her homework, she took her dog for a walk.
2. Mr Wilson marked our test. But he took his dog for a walk first.
   Mr Wilson marked our test after he had taken his dog for a walk.
3. Ella passed her driving test. She bought a car.
   ____
4. She drove home, locked the car and went into the house.
   ____
5. First Ella made a cup of coffee. Then she phoned her friend Anna.
   ____
6. She put down the phone. But first she said goodbye to Anna.
   ____
7. She looked out of the window because she heard a loud noise.
   ____
8. Two young men were trying to steal her car. They broke a window to get into the car.
   ____
9. Ella realised what was happening. She rang the police.
   ____
10. Her neighbour came out of his house. He heard the noise.
    ____
11. The man shouted something. The boys looked up and saw him.
    ____
12. They ran away. A police car arrived outside Ella's house.
    ____

Aufgabe 20

Now join the two sentences with *when*, but remember: sometimes you will need the *past perfect* tense.

1. He told me his name. I knew who he was.

 ____

2. We finished lunch. We went for a walk.

 ____

3. She wiped her feet on the doormat. She shut the front door.

 ____

4. He took the dog for a walk. It was very cold outside.

 ____

5. We finished the test. Our teacher collected our exercise books.

 ____

6. My mum learnt Russian. She went to school in East Germany.

 ____

7. The sun set. The stars came out.

 ____

8. I lit a candle. The lights went out.

 ____

9. He tried to speak French. Everybody laughed.

 ____

10. All my friends were on holiday. I felt very lonely.

 ____

Aufgabe 21

Jane and Alan went on a trip round the USA last July. Here is Jane's diary.

Mon 1	*Flight London – New York: booked into hotel in Manhattan*
Tues 2	*Sightseeing trip round Manhattan: –> Statue of Liberty*
Wed 3	*NYC …*
Thurs 4	*Celebrated Independence Day in New York City!*
Fri 5	*–> by car to Washington*
Sat 6	*Sights of Washington –> Disneyworld (Orlando, Florida)*
Sun 7	
Mon 8	*} Spent 2 days in Florida –> Flew to Arizona*
Tue 9	*Visited Grand Canyon & Yosemite National Park*
Wed 10	
Thurs 11	*} Drove over the Rockies to San Francisco*
Fri 12	*Stayed with friends there*
Sat 13	*Saw Golden Gate Bridge and other sights –> Seattle (plane)*
Sun 14	
Mon 15	*} Two days in Seattle with friends of Alan's –> London via Chicago*
Tue 16	
Wed 17	
Thurs 18	*Recovered from the jet lag (at last!) – felt much better!*

After the trip, Jane told her friends about what they had done. What did she say?
Start like this: ***After we had flown from London to New York, we …***

In some sentences you can use *when* instead of *after*, but not in all of them.

Signalwort *before + past perfect*

Die Kombination ***before + past perfect*** drückt eine erste Handlung aus, die nicht vor Einsetzen der nächsten Handlung beendet werden konnte.

Vergleiche die Sätze.

› I **read** several books about the USA before I **went** there.
She **gave** me the book back **before** she **had finished** it.

He **finished** speaking when/just as three men **rushed** into the room.
Before he **had finished** speaking, three men rushed into the room.

Die Verwendung von *before* und *after* entsprechen dem deutschen Gebrauch von „bevor" und „nachdem".

Aufgabe 22

Join the two sentences with *before* – but be careful! You only need the *past perfect* with *before* if the first action could not be completed before the second action started. Leave out any words in brackets.

1. He couldn't finish his lunch. His guests arrived.
2. She bought a newspaper. The train left.
3. We put warm clothes on. We went out into the snow.
4. The boy jumped off. The bus didn't stop.
5. The TV programme started. We finished our homework.
6. We reached home. Then it began to rain.
7. They didn't reach the bus station (in time). The bus left.
8. She left school. She didn't finish her course.
9. They left New York. They didn't have time to see the Statue of Liberty.
10. We didn't start to eat. The others arrived.

Wann verwende ich das *past perfect progressive*?

1. Für Handlungen in Zeiträumen, die bis in die Gegenwart hineinreichen und die meist mit *for* oder *since* angegeben werden, wird in der Gegenwart das ***present perfect progressive***, in der Vergangenheit das ***past perfect progressive*** verwendet.

   Vergleiche:

   › I **had** just **switched** the TV on when mum **came** in.
   I **had** only **been watching** for five minutes when mum **switched** it off.
   (*direkte Rede*: "Mum! I**'ve** only **been watching** for five minutes!")
   Sue **had been working** there since 2018 when she **met** Colin.
   ("I**'ve been working** here since 2018," Sue said to Colin when they met.)

   Vergleiche auch:

   › I **was watching** TV when mum **came** in and **switched** it off.
   Sue **was working** there when she **met** Colin.

   Hier wird keine Zeitspanne angegeben.

   Die Verlaufsform wird vor allen Dingen bei Verben benutzt, die Handlungen von längerer Dauer ausdrücken: *to live*, *to work*, *to wait*, *to watch*, *to play*, *to listen* usw.

2. Für wiederholte Handlungen in einem ähnlichen Zeitrahmen.

   › He **had been trying** to phone his girlfriend for half an hour before he got through. He said to her, "I**'ve been trying** to phone you for half an hour!"

Im Gegensatz zur ***simple form*** des ***past perfect***, die auf ein fertiges Ergebnis hindeutet, drückt die ***progressive form*** nicht unbedingt aus, dass die Tätigkeit abgeschlossen ist, sondern zeigt eher an, wie man die Zeit zugebracht hat.

› She **had typed** all the letters, so she could go home.
She **had been typing** all afternoon, so she was very tired.

Aufgabe 23

Johnny Brown, a famous pop singer, is giving one of his rare interviews about his career. Look at the reporter's notes of the interview and write the full story. Use the progressive form with *after* or *when* as often as possible. (It isn't always needed.)

Start like this:

Johnny Brown, a famous pop singer, was born in 1984. After he ...

Born 1984.
Left school 2000 – started work as an assistant in a music shop
Learning to play guitar 3 years – joined the Max Miller Band
Left after playing with only two months
Came to live in New York: 2003 – founded The Kriggs 3 years later
Group played together for 2 years – broke up
Solved his drug problem – founded a new group The Days
First concert successful – could only leave stage after six encores*
Made first CD 2012 – fans waited 2 years!
Group worked together 3 years, then broke up in 2014
Gave 20 concerts and made three CDs

* Zugaben

Abschlusstest online 3

Sehr gut! Du hast **Kapitel 3 – Zeitformen der Vergangenheit** durchgearbeitet. Du kannst die verschiedenen Zeitformen der Vergangenheit richtig bilden und verwenden und hast die jeweiligen Signalwörter wiederholt. Auch das Erkennen der zeitlichen Reihenfolge von Abläufen ist kein Problem für dich.

So funktioniert der Abschlusstest online:
Um deinen Lernerfolg zu überprüfen, kannst du nun die Tests online machen. Gehe auf
www.klasse5bis10.klett-lerntraining.de/5X7F
und registriere dich wie vorne im Buch beschrieben.

Welche Tests es gibt, siehst du unten in der Tabelle. Nach jedem Test bekommst du eine Auswertung.

Willst du immer im Blick haben, welche Themen du schon kannst oder was du besser nochmal wiederholen solltest? Dann notiere deine Ergebnisse aus den Abschlusstests in der Tabelle.

Mein Ergebnis im Abschlusstest – Kapitel 3

Thema	Mein Ergebnis
Zeitformen der Vergangenheit	

4 Bedingungssätze

4.1 Bedingungssätze Typ I

Bei einfachen Bedingungen ist die Bedingung leicht zu erfüllen.
Wenn du etwas tust, tritt etwas anderes unweigerlich ein.

Die Zeitenfolge sieht so aus:

If-Satz: *simple present*	Hauptsatz: *will-future*
If you **help** me with my English,	I**'ll help** you with your maths.
… **if** we **invite** them?	**Will** they come to the meeting
… **unless** you **invite** them politely!	They **won't come**

Die Reihenfolge der beiden Satzhälften ist unwichtig.
If … not wird besonders dann durch *unless* ersetzt, wenn das Verb im Hauptsatz verneint ist. So werden Verwirrungen durch die Verneinung des Verbs in beiden Satzhälften vermieden.

Die Verlaufsform der Gegenwart kann auch verwendet werden, um zwischen Dauerhandlung (*progressive*) und „Einmalhandlung" zu unterscheiden.

› If you**'re** really **looking** for a job, you**'ll find** one.

Im *if*-Satz, Typ I, ist das Verb auch im ***present perfect*** möglich.

› If you **have finished** talking, we **will go** on to the next question.

Achtung:
Verwechsle nicht *if* mit *when*! Im Deutschen wird beides mit „wenn" übersetzt.

Aufgabe 1

Look at the pictures and use them to complete the sentences below. Sometimes you have to provide the *if*-clause, sometimes the main clause.

1. If I ever go to America, ______________________________________.
2. We'll come to your party ____________________________________.
3. Unless it rains, ____________________________ barbecue outside.
4. Our friends won't come unless _______________________________.
5. Will you lend me £10 ________________________ back on Tuesday?
6. If you don't understand English, you ________ not _______ these books.
7. _______________ me do the washing-up if I ___________________ ______________________________?
8. I'll go to Spain in the summer ____________________ enough money.
9. Unless we ___________________ faster, the others _________ us!

Bedingungssätze Typ I mit modalen Hilfsverben im Hauptsatz

Beim einfachen Bedingungssatz Typ I drückt die Zukunftsform im Hauptsatz aus, dass bei Erfüllung der Bedingung das Ergebnis immer eintritt.
Mit dem Einsatz anderer modaler Hilfsverben im Hauptsatz (statt *will* z. B. *can*, *may*, *might* usw.) können statt der 100%igen Sicherheit des Ergebnisses andere „Modalitäten" (Können, Möglichkeit usw.) ausgedrückt werden.

Vergleiche den einfachen Bedingungssatz Typ I

If we go to New York, we**'ll visit** Manhattan. (100 % certain)

mit:

If we visit Manhattan, we **can** go to the top of the Empire State Building. (ability)

If we go to the Empire State Building, we **could** have lunch there. (less likely)

If we have enough time, we **may** visit Harlem. (possibility)

But if we visit Harlem, we **might** see a film star. (less likely)

If you are alone in New York, you **must** be careful. (necessity)

But if you wear your oldest clothes, you **needn't** worry about getting dirty. (no necessity)

You **should** be/**ought to** be safe enough unless you go out in the dark. (probability)

If you don't know a person, you **shouldn't** trust him or her. (advice)

If you remember, **could** you buy me a few postcards of New York? (request)

Aufgabe 2

Read the dialogue and put in modal auxiliaries to suit the context.

1. What are your plans for the weekend, Samira?
   – Well, if the weather is good, Dad says we ________________ go for a drive in the country on Saturday.
2. That's one possibility. What about a trip to the seaside?
   – I suppose we ________________ go to Eastbourne if we start early enough. It's a long way, though. What about your plans, Rosie?
3. I haven't got any. Do you think you ________________ take me with you if you go to Eastbourne? I haven't been to the seaside for ages.
4. I'll ask Mum and Dad. If there's room in the car, that ________________ be all right.
5. Will we have time to go to the top of those high cliffs?
   – You mean Beachy Head? I'm not sure. We ________________ have time if we don't spend too long on the beach.
6. But if we go right to the top, you ________________ be very careful! It's very dangerous.
7. Will we be back before it gets dark?
   – I expect so. We ______________ get stuck in a traffic jam if we're very unlucky, but that's not very likely. Should I phone you on Friday evening?
8. No, that won't be necessary. If your parents say I can come, you ________________ phone me. When should I be at your house?
9. Come round after breakfast. If you arrive at about ten, we ____________ leave straight away.
10. We ________________ leave much later than ten if we want to get back before dark.

4.2 Bedingungssätze Typ II

Bei Sätzen des Typs II ist die Bedingung oft unerfüllbar: Wenn du etwas tätest, träte eventuell etwas anderes ein.
Viele Aussagen des Typs II verbleiben im Bereich des Wunschdenkens.

Die Zeitenfolge sieht so aus:

If-Satz: *simple past* (eigentlich Konjunktiv)	Hauptsatz: *would* + Infinitiv (conditional)
If I **had** a bit more time,	I **would read** that magazine.
… if it **didn't rain** so much!	We**'d spend** our holidays in England
If they **knew** the right answer,	**would** they **tell** us?
If the money **was found**	we **would give** them a reward.

Die Reihenfolge der beiden Satzhälften ist unwichtig. Oft wird guter Rat mit der einzigen noch vorhandenen, englischen Konjunktivform ausgedrückt.

› If I **were** you, I **wouldn't wait** for the bus. It's quicker to walk.

Auch die ***progressive form*** und andere Hilfsverben in beiden Satzhälften (vgl. Kap. 4.1) sind möglich.

› If I **were** in the office now, I **would be working** hard.
If I **were learning** Spanish, I **might go** to Spain.
If my car **were working**, I **could drive** you home.
If only I **could speak** more French, I **wouldn't worry** about moving to Paris.

Aufgabe 3

Be careful not to mix Type I and Type II sentences.

Put the halves of the sentences together.

1. If the boat sinks,
2. Unless you behave,
3. If you stole a car,
4. If our teacher is ill,
5. If the bus didn't come,
6. If the school burned down,
7. Will you phone me
8. Would you help them
9. She'll lend you her book
10. I'd be more careful

a) you would be punished.
b) we'd have to walk to school.
c) we wouldn't be sorry.
d) I won't let you go to the party.
e) we'll have to swim.
f) we won't have a test tomorrow.
g) if you knew they needed help?
h) if I were you!
i) if you have time?
j) if you ask nicely.

Aufgabe 4

Complete the sentences with the right form of the verb in brackets.

1. **(visit)** If you are a visitor to Australia, you ________ probably ______________ the Great Barrier Reef.
2. **(see)** If you went diving, you ___________ an amazing underwater world.
3. **(be)** You would probably migrate there if you ______________ an animal.
4. **(go)** ________ you ______________ there if you knew the future of this paradise was in danger?
5. **(see)** If you looked at old photos of the reef, you ______________ that most of the coral has disappeared.
6. **(not be)** There wouldn't be coral bleaching if it ______________ for climate change and warmer water.
7. **(not be)** There ______________ so much waste from birds if there weren't the snorkelling platforms for tourists.
8. **(not pollute)** If the birds waste wasn't in the water, it ______________ it.
9. **(not happen)** If ships weren't allowed there, oil spills and accidents and damage the reef.
10. **(visit)** ________ you ______________ the Great Barrier Reef if you visited Australia?

4.3 Bedingungssätze Typ III

Wenn du etwas getan hättest, wäre etwas anderes eingetreten (oder auch nicht). Da die Bedingung sowieso unerfüllbar ist, verbleiben alle Aussagen der Bedingungssätze des Typs III im Bereich des Wunschdenkens bzw. der verpassten Gelegenheiten.

Die Zeitenfolge sieht so aus:

If-Satz: *past perfect* (eigentlich Konjunktiv)	Hauptsatz: *would have* + *past participle* (= *conditional perfect*)
If I **had known** you were coming,	I'**d have baked** a cake.
… if I'**d had** enough of my own.	I **wouldn't have asked** you for money
… if you **had been** in my shoes?	What **would** you **have done**

Die ***progressive form*** ist auch möglich.

› If you **had been paying** attention, you **would have noticed** the mistake.

Die Reihenfolge der beiden Satzhälften ist unwichtig.

Bei den Wörtern *hätte* und *wäre* musst du aufpassen!

› Wenn er mir das gleich **gesagt hätte**, **hätte** ich ihm **verziehen**.
*If he **had told** me that right away, I **would have forgiven** him.*

„Hätte" bleibt *had* im *if*-Satzteil, weil es sich um eine echte Konjunktivform handelt. Im Hauptsatz aber stellt „hätte" eine Verschmelzung von „würde … haben" dar. Im Englischen wird die unverkürzte Konstruktion *would have* benutzt.

Dasselbe gilt für „wäre", denn die zusammengesetzten Perfektformen werden im Englischen alle mit *have* gebildet.

› Wenn wir früher **gekommen wären**, **wären** wir auch früher **gegangen**.
*If we **had arrived** earlier, we **would have left** earlier too.*

Aufgabe 5

Read the following blog post about volunteer work in India and pick out the *if*-sentences. Put them into separate lists for Types I, II and III.

You may shorten the longer sentences.

Working as a volunteer in India

If you had asked me a year ago, what I would have done after school my answer would have probably been, 'I'll go to university and study Business Studies if I get the right marks'. So much has changed since my final year at school. Let me tell you.

My name is Claire Palmer and I'm 19 years old. I took part in a volunteer project in India where I made new friends and I was surprised how much I learned about myself.

If you want to find a volunteer project, you will find so much information on the internet. There is probably too much information but if you know roughly what you want to do, it will make things easier. I knew I wanted to work with children and there were a number of projects in orphanages teaching children. I worked for three months, and it was very hard to leave all the children after that time.

There is a lot to organise before you start your project. If you thought I was just talking about booking your flight and packing your suitcase, you would be very wrong. Depending on the country you are going to you will need to have vaccinations and organise important papers, you have to pay the organisation who runs the project, and you have to pay for your own travel and personal expenses. You would be advised to get a weekend or part-time job if you haven't got one. I worked in a local supermarket and with some help from my parents I had the money when my contract arrived. I would have asked my grandparents for a loan, if I hadn't saved enough money, but I didn't need to which was great.

India was a complete surprise. It was hot and noisy, and the smells as we drove past the food stalls in the street were amazing. Everyone was really helpful and if I had had any problems, I would have known who to go to. I lived with a host family and was homesick at the beginning and thought, 'If I don't feel better soon, I'll have to change my flight and go home.' My homesick didn't last long and the three months flew past, and it was time to leave.

If you do a volunteer project, you'll never forget it. If I got the chance, I would volunteer for the same project again.

Aufgabe 6

Look at the pictures and tell the story. This is a chain exercise (the second half of one sentence gives you the first half of the next). Start like this:

1. *John had a scooter with old tyres. If he had listened to his friend Richie, he would have bought new tyres before going on holiday.*
2. *If he had bought new tyres, ...*
3. *If he hadn't had ...*

4.4 Mischformen

Manchmal haben Ereignisse in der Vergangenheit Auswirkungen in der Gegenwart. Das führt zu den folgenden Mischformen.

Typ II + I

If you **enjoyed** Dragon Quest,
(= when you first played it)

you **will love** our new game.
(= now)

You will not **remember** me
(= now)

… unless you **were** at Brighton.
(= last year)

If they **have** never **met**,
(= so far)

they **won't know** each other.
(= now)

Typ III + II

Would she **be** a famous film star today
(= result in the present)

… if she **hadn't met** Steven Spielberg in 1990?
(= meeting in the past)

In beiden Satzteilen kann auch die Verlaufsform verwendet werden.

If only I **had listened** to you,
(= advice given in the past)

I **would be living** in luxury now!
(= result in the present)

She **would know** the answer

… if she **had been paying** attention.

Achtung: Verwechsle nicht *if* mit *when*! Im Deutschen wird beides mit „wenn" übersetzt:

I'll phone you **when** I return.
I'll phone you **if** I return.

Ich rufe dich an, **wenn** ich zurückkomme.

Im Englischen gibt der Nebensatz mit *when* im Beispielsatz den **Zeitpunkt** des Anrufes an, während der Nebensatz mit *if* die **Bedingung** nennt, unter der überhaupt ein Anruf erfolgt.

Aufgabe 7

Put the two sentences together. Use the *progressive forms* where necessary.

1. She didn't fail her exams. She isn't repeating a year.
   If she had failed her exams, she would be repeating a year.
2. I didn't win a prize. I am very unhappy.
3. John is living in London now. He found a job there last year.
4. My friend started learning French a couple of years ago. He spends his holidays there regularly.
5. Did you like the group's last CD? You'll love this one!
6. You don't know Alice? Weren't you at my party last year?
7. He emigrated to Australia when he was a boy. He is a wealthy farmer now.
8. She learned to speak Arabic when she was a girl. She is working in Beirut now.
9. You bought your mountain bike three years ago? You need a new one now!
10. How will you recognise him? You've never seen him before!
11. Have they ever been there? – No, they don't know the place.

Aufgabe 8

Join the two halves of the sentences with *if* or *when*.

1. We can have a break		you want to learn French.
2. She'll pass her exams		she could speak Spanish.
3. I might go to Venezuela		we are 18.
4. You should talk to Jean		my parents pay for my ticket.
5. They could go to Spain	if when	he'll be arriving.
6. We can get married		they aren't too hard.
7. She'd get a better job		the flights are cheap.
8. I have no idea		this exercise is done.
9. You'll remember him		you see him again.

Abschlusstest online 4

Glückwunsch! Du hast **Kapitel 4 – Bedingungssätze** durchgearbeitet. Du hast die unterschiedlichen *if-clauses* wiederholt, und weißt, auf welche Fallen du nicht hereinfallen darfst. Du kannst Wünsche äußern und ausdrücken, was „gewesen wäre, wenn …".
Außerdem verwendest du die kniffeligen Mischformen der Bedingungssätze sicher.

So funktioniert der Abschlusstest online:
Um deinen Lernerfolg zu überprüfen, kannst du nun die Tests online machen. Gehe auf
www.klasse5bis10.klett-lerntraining.de/5X7F
und registriere dich wie vorne im Buch beschrieben.

Welche Tests es gibt, siehst du unten in der Tabelle. Nach jedem Test bekommst du eine Auswertung.

Willst du immer im Blick haben, welche Themen du schon kannst oder was du besser nochmal wiederholen solltest? Dann notiere deine Ergebnisse aus den Abschlusstests in der Tabelle.

Mein Ergebnis im Abschlusstest – Kapitel 4

Thema	Mein Ergebnis
Bedingungssätze	

5 Die indirekte Rede

5.1 Befehle in der indirekten Rede

Direkte Rede	**Indirekte Rede**

1. Die Befehlsform (Imperativ) in der direkten Rede wird in der indirekten Rede mit einem Infinitiv wiedergegeben. Es spielt keine Rolle, ob das Einführungsverb in einer Zeitform der Gegenwart oder Vergangenheit steht.

"**Stop** talking!"	Our teacher often **tells** us **to stop** talking. Yesterday he **told** us **to stop** talking twice.
"**Don't talk**!"	He **has asked** us **not to talk** several times. I **asked** you **not to talk** five minutes ago!

2. Aufforderungsverstärkungen bzw. -abschwächungen (*For goodness sake …!*, *Please don't …*) werden nicht in die indirekte Rede übernommen, sondern durch ein kräftiges bzw. mildes Einführungsverb ausgedrückt. Diese Verben reichen vom „Betteln" bis hin zum „Brüllen".

"**For goodness sake don't lose** your tickets!"	Our teacher **begged** us **not to lose** our tickets.
"**Please be** quiet!"	He **requested**/**asked** us to be quiet.
"**Be** prepared!"	She **warned**/**told** them **to be** prepared.
"***Do* shut** up, Chris!"	I **ordered** Chris **to shut** up.
"**Take** cover!!"	The man **roared** at us **to take** cover.

3. Vergiss nicht, dass ein verneinter Befehl nicht immer mit "*Don't …*" ausgedrückt wird.

"**Never leave** the door unlocked!"	She told us **never to leave** the door unlocked.

Direkte Rede	**Indirekte Rede**

4. Wenn es sich weniger um Befehle als um einen guten Rat handelt, sind *recommend* oder *advise* geeignete Einführungsverben.

"**Don't eat** the fish!"	She **advised**/**recommended** me **not to eat** the fish.
"**Try** this ice cream!"	He **recommended** us **to try** the/this ice cream.

In fast allen Fällen muss die Person, an die der direkte Befehl gerichtet wird, in der indirekten Rede erwähnt werden.

Aufgabe 1

Make complete sentences out of the following direct commands. Be careful! The "command" given in sentence 12 is not given by people.

1. "Fasten your seatbelts, please."

   The flight attendant asked the passengers to fasten their seatbelts.
2. "Please stop talking!"
3. "Empty your pockets!"
4. "Abandon ship!"
5. "Follow that car!"
6. "Wash this T-shirt in warm water only."
7. "Don't hit your sister!"
8. "Always look over your shoulder when reversing."
9. "Never come into the gym with street shoes!"
10. "Be quiet and sit down!"
11. "Meet me at the station."
12. BUY RILEY MOTOR CARS!
13. "For goodness sake don't drive so fast!"
14. "Put up your hands and stand perfectly still!"
15. "Fire!"
16. "Do pay attention, please!"

Aufgabe 2

Look at the pictures and tell the story. Use the *simple past* with a suitable introductory verb for each situation – "asked, begged, told, requested, warned", etc.

Start like this:

1. Yesterday Kate's mother ______________ rice and a few other things.

2. Her little brother Tommy ______________________________

____.

3. Kate agreed (= "OK …"), but ______________________________

____.

4. In the shop Kate ______________________________

____.

5. Then Tommy ______________________________

____

an ice lolly, but Kate said no.

6. Tommy started to cry, but Kate ______________________________

____.

7. After that, Kate ______________________________

____.

8. But Tommy was angry and pulled one of the shelves over.

The shopkeeper ______________________________

____.

9. Then the shopkeeper ______________________________

____.

10. Outside, Kate ______________________________

____.

5.2 Aussagen in der indirekten Rede

Aussagen in der indirekten Rede

1. Wird die indirekte Rede mit einem Verb im ***simple present*** bzw. ***present perfect*** eingeleitet, werden alle Zeitformen „unverschoben" übernommen.

"I **live** in London now, but I **lived** in York for three years. We **have been living** in England since I **was** three, so I **can** speak English like a native. But we **are** German, and we **will be returning** to Germany soon."	Anna **says** (that) she **lives** in London now, but that she **lived** in York for three years. She and her family **have been living** in England since she **was** three, so she **can** speak English like a native. But they **are** German, and **will be returning** to Germany soon.
"Jana **doesn't like** Munich. She **moved** there because of her job. After she **had been living** there for a week she **wanted** to go home."	Nils **has** just **told** me that his girlfriend Jana **doesn't like** Munich. She **moved** there because of her job. After she **had been living** there for a week she **wanted** to go home.

2. Wird die indirekte Rede mit einem Verb im ***simple past*** bzw. ***past perfect*** eingeleitet, müssen alle Zeitformen der direkten Rede um eine Zeitform nach hinten in die Vergangenheit verschoben werden. Bei Zeitformen, die mit Hilfsverben gebildet werden, wird nur das Hilfsverb verschoben.

"I **live** in London now, but I **lived** in York for three years. We **have been living** in England since I **was** three, so I **can** speak English like a native. But we **are** German, and we **will be returning** to Germany soon."	Anna **said** (that) she **lived** in London now, but that she **had lived** in York for three years. She went on to say that she and her family **had been living** in England since she **had been** three, so she **could** speak English like a native. But she explained that they **were** German, and **would be returning** to Germany soon.

"Jana **doesn't like** Munich. She **moved** there because of her job. After she **had been living** there for a week she **wanted** to go home."

After Nils **had told** me that his girlfriend Jana **didn't like** Munich and **had moved** there because of her job, I asked him what her plans were. He **said** that after she **had been living** in Munich for a week she **had wanted** to go home.

Aufgabe 3

a) **Are you a good interpreter? Your friend from Germany can understand some English but is very shy and can't speak much English yet, so you have to help him/her. Some of your friends want to know about life in Germany. Translate your friend's answers. Start every sentence with "He/She says (that) ..."**

1. Where do you live? – In der Nähe von Dortmund.
   He/She says he/she lives near Dortmund.
2. Do you live in a house or a flat? – In einer Wohnung.
3. What sort of music do you like? – Techno.
4. Have you got any brothers or sisters? – Zwei Brüder und eine Schwester.
5. What are your hobbies? – Fußball und Skateboarding.
6. Do you play football at school? – Nein, ich spiele in einem Fußballverein.
7. Do you still go to school on Saturdays? – Nein – nicht mehr.
8. Have you ever been to America? – Nein – noch nicht.
9. When did you start learning English? – Erst (= *only*) vor einem Jahr.
10. Do you like it over here? – Ja!
11. When are you going back to Germany? – In zwei Wochen.
12. What were you doing yesterday afternoon? – Ich spielte Fußball.
13. Yes, I saw you in the park. Who was that girl with you? – Das ist Mia. Sie kommt auch aus Dortmund. Sie kam zum Fußballplatz, nachdem sie ihre Hausaufgaben gemacht hatte.

b) **The next day you have to report what was said. Use the sentences from a) and start like this: "He/She said ...".**

1. *He/She said he/she lived near Dortmund.*

Orts- und Zeitangaben

Wenn du etwas wiedergibst, ist es oft, aber nicht immer, notwendig, Orts- und Zeitangaben zu ändern.

› "I was **here yesterday**"
= He said he had been **there the previous day**/**the day before**.

Die häufigsten Umstellungen sind:

direct	indirect	direct	indirect
here	there	tomorrow	the next/following day
this	that	yesterday	the previous day/ the day before
these	those		
today	that day	next week/month/year	the following week …
		last week/month/year	the previous week …
		a year/month/week ago	a year/month … before

Aufgabe 4

Report the following commands and statements to suit the times and places given. Make any other changes necessary.

1. "Meet me **here tomorrow**." (It's Monday morning. I am in Cardiff.)
   (It's Monday evening. I am in Cardiff.) ***He told me to meet him here tomorrow***.
   (It's Tuesday. I am in London.) ***He told me to meet him there/in Cardiff today***.
2. "I will be flying **to London tomorrow**." (Berlin, Tuesday)
   (Berlin, Wednesday a.m.) ***Yesterday she told me that she would be flying to London today***.
3. "I'm staying here tonight." (Leeds, Sunday a.m.)
   a) (Leeds, Sunday p.m.) She said …
   b) (Leeds, Monday a.m.) She told me yesterday morning …
   c) (London, Tuesday) On Sunday she informed me that …
4. "I saw John in London yesterday." (York, Tuesday)
   a) (London, Wednesday) Peter told me …
   b) (York, Friday) Peter told me …
   c) (London, Tuesday) Peter rang me and said …

Befehle und Aussagen

Manchmal muss man eine Kombination von Befehlen und Aussagen in der indirekten Rede wiedergeben. Ist eine Aufforderung begründet, brauchst du ein Einführungsverb für den Befehl und *because* für die Aussage.

› "Clean your bike! It's dirty."
= He **told** me to clean my bike **because** it was dirty.

Manchmal ist ein Befehl die Folge einer Situation oder Handlung. Dann kann man den Befehlsteil mit *so* einbinden.

› Dad: "It's a special occasion." Mum: "Wear your best clothes."
= Dad said it was a special occasion, **so** Mum told us to wear our best clothes.

Oft ist aber keine Begründung vorhanden, und hier brauchst du zwei unterschiedliche Einführungsverben.

› "Wake up! I've got a surprise for you."
= My mum **told** me to wake up and **said** that she had got a surprise for me.

Aufgabe 5

Say what happened. Use an introductory verb in the *past tense*.

1. *Friend:* "Be quiet! I'm thinking!"
   My friend told me to be quiet because he was thinking.
2. *Teacher:* "I have to go and see the headteacher. Take out your books and do the exercise on page 23."
3. *Mother:* "Give me your dirty jeans. I want to wash them."
4. *Brother:* "I lent you £2. Give it me back!"
5. *Sister:* "Take that T-shirt off! It's mine!"
6. *Friend:* "Have another biscuit. I've got plenty."
7. *Police officer:* "This road has been flooded. Follow the DIVERSION signs."
8. *Uncle:* "Come in and sit down. Have a cup of tea. I wasn't expecting you so early."
9. *Ticket inspector:* "This ticket is only valid with a Young Person's Railcard. Show me your Railcard, please."
10. *Ex-boyfriend:* "Go home! I didn't invite you to my party!"
11. *Notice:* Avoid the last-minute rush. Post early for Christmas.

5.3 Fragen in der indirekten Rede

Fragen ohne Fragewort

Bei Fragen unterscheidet man allgemein zwischen Fragen mit oder ohne Fragewort (*Who? When? How?* usw.). Das gilt auch in der indirekten Rede. Hier geht es zunächst um Fragen ohne Fragewort.

1. Mit Frageverb *Do/Does – Did*

› "**Does** he **like** ice cream?"
She **asks** me **if** he **likes** ice cream.
She **asked** me **if** he **liked** ice cream.

"**Did** he **know** the answer?"
She **wants** to know **if** he **knew** the answer.
She **wanted** to know **if** he **had known** the answer.

Die Fragebildung mit *Do/Does – Did* wird durch *if/whether* ersetzt, wobei natürlich die entsprechenden Änderungen in Verbform (z. B. 3.-Person-*s* in der Gegenwart) und Zeitform (*"Did she know"* = *… if she knew*) vorgenommen werden müssen.
Die Verschiebung der Zeitformen ist die gleiche wie bei Aussagesätzen.

2. Mit Hilfsverb

› "**May** I **open** a window?"
I **asked** him **if**/**whether** I **might** open a window.
"**Are** they **going** to the party? **Will** John **be** there too?"
She **asked if** they **were going** to the party and **if** John **would be** there too.
"**Have** you **come** by car? **Can** you **give** me a lift?"
He **asked** me **if** I **had come** by car and **whether** I **could give** him a lift.
"**Hadn't** we better call an ambulance?"
They **wondered whether** they **hadn't** better call an ambulance.

Hier steht das Frageverb in der entsprechenden Zeitform nach der Einleitung mit *if/whether*. Die Umstellung Hilfsverb – Subjekt wird aufgehoben.
Signalwörter: *if*, *whether* (= ob)
Bei *whether* schwingt die Bedeutung „… oder vielleicht auch nicht“ mit, *if* ist ganz neutral.

Aufgabe 6

a) **Put the two halves of the sentences together. Be careful with the tenses!**

1. I want to know if
2. She wanted to find out whether
3. He asked me if
4. Our teacher sometimes asks if
5. The man asked her whether
6. My mother wants to know if
7. The driver inquired whether
8. He wondered if
9. They wanted to know if
10. I wonder whether

a) I knew the right answer.
b) she had seen his umbrella.
c) the hotel had a good garage.
d) his parents knew where he was.
e) the water is warm enough for swimming.
f) this exercise is difficult.
g) their son had received their letter yet.
h) we do our homework on the bus.
i) you'll be staying for supper.
j) she could get a bus to Chelsham.

b) **First check that your answers are correct. Then write the actual questions.**

1. *Is this exercise difficult?*

Fragen mit Fragewort

Bei Fragen mit einem Fragewort wird anstelle von *if/whether* das Fragewort selbst wiederholt. **Signalwörter**: *Who, What, When, Where, Why, How, How much, How often*, usw.

1. Mit *Who/What* als Subjekt
   Wenn *Who/What* als Subjekt der Frage benutzt wird, gibt es kaum Änderungen. Es muss nur die entsprechende Zeitform benutzt werden.
   › "**Who knows** the answer?"
   Our teacher **wants to know who knows** the answer.
   Our teacher **wanted to know who knew** the answer.
   "**What lives** in trees and is dangerous?"
   He **asked** me **what lived** in trees and **was** dangerous, so I told him, "A crow with a gun."

2. Mit Fragewort + *do/does/did*
   Do/does/did als fragebildendes Verb entfällt. Es gelten die entsprechenden Zeitverschiebungen.
   › "**Where** do you **live**?"
   He **is asking** you **where** you **live**.
   She **asked** me **where** I **lived**.
   "**How much did** those jeans cost?"
   "I **want to know how much** your jeans **cost**!"
   My mother **wanted to know how much** my jeans **had cost**.
   "**Who(m) do** you **know** in London?"
   She **asked** me **who(m)** I **knew** in London.

3. Mit Fragewort + anderen Hilfsverben
   Das Hilfsverb wird in die für das Einführungsverb entsprechende Zeitform verschoben.
   › "**Why can't** you **come**?"
   Why **is** he **asking** me **why** I **can't come**?
   He **asked** me why I **couldn't come**.
   "**How much has** that man **told** you?"
   They **wanted to know how much** the man **had told** me.

Aufgabe 7

Put these questions into indirect speech. Use the introductions given.

1. "Who left the front door open?!"

   My father asked me ______________________________

2. "What are you doing here?"

   She wants to know ______________________________

3. "How much money have you got?"

   His friend asked her ______________________________

4. "How many prisoners had escaped before the prison staff found the hole?"

   The reporter requested information about ______________________________

   ____

5. "When did the football match take place?"

   He wants to know ______________________________

6. "How soon can you repair my car?"

   The motorist asked the mechanic ______________________________

7. "What's happened to John?"

   Our youth leader wanted to know ______________________________

8. "How far is Reading from London?"

   One of the tourists has just asked ______________________________

9. "Where do flies go in the winter?"

   The child asked his mother ______________________________

10. "What did you do after you had left the hotel?"

    The police officer asked me ______________________________

    ____

Aufgabe 8

Here is a mixed bag of commands, statements and questions. Put them into indirect speech. You may need different introductory verbs (if you have a question and a statement to report) or a change of verb for stylistic reasons.
Always use introductory verbs in the *simple past* and the characters suggested in brackets.

1. "Turn left here. My house is on the right." **(driving instructor – me)**
   The driving instructor told me to turn left (here) and informed me that his house was on the right.
2. "Wake up! What's the matter with you?" **(mum – son)**
3. "I love French wine. Pass me the bottle!" **(Kieran – Peter)**
4. "Does Marc like wine too? Let's offer him some." **(Peter)**
5. "Pay attention! I have to tell you everything twice." **(teacher – student)**
6. "Come here, Robin! Where did you get those sausages? You're a bad dog!" **(Tania – her dog Robin)**
7. "Are you Janet Smith?" – "Yes" – "Good. Come in and sit down. Have a coffee." **(manager of the firm – project manager)**
8. "I was surprised not to see you at Phil's party. Where were you last night? Tell me the truth." **(Anna – her boyfriend Malek)**
9. "Let's wait a few minutes longer. I've no idea where the others have got to. Do you think they're lost?" **(Oliver – me)**
10. "Stop! There's a red light! Why can't you drive more carefully?" **(driving instructor – my sister/brother)**
11. "Let's finish this exercise and have a break." – "A good idea." **(teacher – me)**

Abschlusstest online 5

Prima! Du hast **Kapitel 5 – Die indirekte Rede** durchgearbeitet. Dabei hast du wiederholt, wann sich die Zeitformen verschieben und ob sich Zeit- und Ortsangaben ändern. Du kannst jetzt gut von der direkten in die indirekte Rede wechseln. Auch Fragen in der indirekten Rede kannst du korrekt formulieren.

So funktioniert der Abschlusstest online:
Um deinen Lernerfolg zu überprüfen, kannst du nun die Tests online machen.
Gehe auf
www.klasse5bis10.klett-lerntraining.de/5X7F
und registriere dich wie vorne im Buch beschrieben.

Welche Tests es gibt, siehst du unten in der Tabelle. Nach jedem Test bekommst du eine Auswertung.

Willst du immer im Blick haben, welche Themen du schon kannst oder was du besser nochmal wiederholen solltest? Dann notiere deine Ergebnisse aus den Abschlusstests in der Tabelle.

Mein Ergebnis im Abschlusstest – Kapitel 5

Thema	Mein Ergebnis
Indirekte Rede	

6 Partizipien – Gerundium – Infinitiv

6.1 Partizipien als Adjektive und zur Verkürzung von Relativsätzen

Partizipien als Adjektive

Active
The room has **running** water.
*Das Zimmer hat **fließendes** Wasser.*
This book is **interesting**.
*Dieses Buch ist **interessant**.*

Passive
We like **baked** beans.
*Wir essen gerne **gebackene** Bohnen.*
I am **interested** in history.
*Ich bin an Geschichte **interessiert**.*

Partizipien zur Verkürzung von Relativsätzen

Zur Verkürzung von Relativkonstruktionen werden Partizipien so verwendet:

Present participle
ersetzt eine aktive Zeitform.

The girl **who is sitting** there is my sister.
The girl **sitting** there is my sister.

I picked up the book **which lay** on the table.
I picked up the book **lying** on the table.

Past participle
ersetzt eine passive Zeitform.

The man **who was seen** near the station was the thief.
The man **seen** near the station was the thief.
The building **which was painted** last week is the bus station.
The building **painted** last week is the bus station.

Aufgabe 1

Use the correct participle form of the green words to complete these sentences.

1. What are your **interests**? – I'm … pop music and American football. I think they're very … .
2. What **frightened** your friend? – He saw a ghost. It was a very … experience for him. He's always been … of the dark.
3. How long do you **boil** your eggs? – That depends. If you leave them longer than three minutes in … water, you get hard-… eggs.
4. When we arrived the rain was **falling**. We couldn't sleep because of the sound of … rain, and the next morning the grass was covered with … leaves.
5. Have you **booked** tickets for the rock concert yet? Last time you forgot and the concert was fully … . – I must go down to the … office this afternoon.
6. Examinations **terrify** me. – You needn't be … of your end-of-term tests. There's nothing … about them!
7. Why are you **wearing** your oldest jeans? They look so old and … out!

Aufgabe 2

Read the following story and write down all the *relative clauses* (which have been) shortened in the above ways.

Dropping your aitches

When I was a boy many people living in London spoke English with a Cockney accent. Originally, Cockney was the dialect spoken by people born in the East End of London: within hearing distance of the church bells of St Mary-le-Bow (known by Londoners simply as Bow Bells). Foreigners – or even many other Britons – listening to a real Cockney sometimes have great difficulty in understanding what he or she is saying. One of the things which makes understanding Cockney difficult is that Cockneys often leave out the h at the beginning of words. A Cockney saying, "'ave you 'ad any 'elp with this exercise?" is really saying, "Have you had any help with this exercise?" Cockneys educated at grammar schools try to avoid this "dropping of aitches", but sometimes someone less well educated puts a missing aitch in front of a word where it is not needed, and the result is: "Have you had hany help with this hexercise?"

Aufgabe 3

Use a participle construction to shorten the *relative clauses* in these sentences.

1. The girl **who lives** next door met me in the street.

   ***The girl** living **next door met me in the street**.*
2. The man who is standing over there looks familiar.
3. Which man? The one who is wearing the long raincoat?
4. No. The one who is dressed in those dirty old jeans and a pullover.
5. Yes. Isn't he the man who was wanted by the police for that bank robbery?
6. Don't be silly, Anne! Doesn't he remind you of the man who lives in the flat upstairs?
7. You mean Mr Phillips? He doesn't wear clothes like that! He works at that bank which is situated right opposite my office. I see him every day.
8. Not Mr Phillips! The other man – the one who was invited to Jane's party last week. What's his name?
9. I don't know. I didn't go to her party. But I know who you mean. He looks a bit like one of the men who work at the Station Garage. Perhaps that's why he's dressed like that.
10. Can't you remember his name? – It's a Scottish name which begins with Mac.
11. McTavish? … McDougall … Macintosh? – No. What's the name of that chain of restaurants which sells hamburgers and things?

Aufgabe 4

Look at the pictures on page 93 and say what is happening. You should use a participle to shorten your sentences.

1. The man sitting at the table is reading the paper.
or: The man reading the paper is sitting at the table.

Neben den beiden bisher geübten Funktionen spielen die Partizipien eine wichtige stilistische Rolle, besonders im geschriebenen Englisch.
In der gesprochenen Sprache kann man zwei Hauptsätze durchaus mit *and* verbinden. Beim Schreiben kann man etwas mehr am Satzgefüge „feilen".

› "We looked at the menu **and** found that the food was quite expensive."
Looking at the menu, we found that the food was quite expensive.

6.2 Partizipien zur Verkürzung anderer Satzarten

Englisch	**Deutsch**
Zwei Hauptsätze (beide Handlungen gleichzeitig)	
› She looked at her watch **and** saw that it was late. **Looking** at her watch, she saw that it was late.	Sie schaute auf ihre Uhr und sah …
Nebensätze mit Zeitbestimmung (eine Handlung vor der anderen)	
› **After** he **had had** a good meal, he felt better. **Having had** a good meal, he felt better.	**Nachdem** er … **gehabt hatte**, …
Manchmal muss du die Konjunktion beibehalten, um den Zeitbezug deutlich auszudrücken.	
› **While waiting** for the bus, he read the paper.	**Während** er …
When told that the police knew where he was, he left town.	**Als** ihm **gesagt wurde**, …
After having had a good meal, he felt better.	**Nachdem** er … **gehabt hatte**, …
Until told by his friends, he had no idea that he snored.	**Bis** es ihm seine Freunde **sagten**, …
Nebensätze mit Begründung (*because*, *as*, *since*)	
› **As/Because** he knew the answer, he put up his hand. **Knowing** the answer, he put up his hand.	**Da/Weil** er die Antwort wusste, …
Since she **didn't** wish to get involved, she … **Not wishing** to get involved, she said nothing.	**Da** sie **nicht** darin verwickelt werden wollte, …
Nebensätze mit Bedingungen (*if*, *unless*) oder (seltener) bei Einräumungen (*although*, *though*)	
› **If** the meat is kept in a fridge, it will stay fresh. The meat will stay fresh **if kept** in a fridge.	**Wenn** …
You must keep on walking **unless** you are told to stop. You must keep on walking **unless told** to stop.	**Wenn** … **nicht** …
Although we live here, we don't know the place well. **Though living** here we don't know the place well.	**Obwohl** …

Achtung: Das Subjekt muss in beiden Sätzen das gleiche sein!

Aufgabe 5

Shorten the following sentences using participles, but only where possible! Beware of unrelated participles (Partizipien, die sich nicht auf das Satzsubjekt beziehen!). Change these sentences if you can think of a way to do so, or leave them unchanged.

1. I walked across the room and shut the door.
2. When we had listened to the new song, we went out for a hamburger.
3. Because he did not know the way he asked a passerby.
4. As she wanted to go to the cinema, her boyfriend changed his plans.
5. Unless they are taught English properly, they will not be able to get good jobs abroad.
6. When passengers leave the train, they should take all their luggage with them.
7. Stay calm if you are stopped by a police officer.
8. Though it is made in Korea, this car is still very good.
9. The headteacher walked into the room and we all stopped talking.
10. The headteacher walked into the room and sat down at the teacher's table.
11. She had no worries until they told her she had to leave the country within 48 hours.
12. John went to Oxford after he had got four A's in his A-levels.

Aufgabe 6

Now put these pairs of sentences together using the above constructions. In sentences followed by (2), two sentences are possible – please give both.

1. He shut the door. He sat down.
2. I passed my driving test. I bought a car.
3. She sat in the bath. She read a newspaper. (2)
4. We didn't want to go. So we stayed at home.
5. I didn't learn French at school. I wasn't able to read the letter.
6. My friend fell asleep. He was watching TV.
7. She did not live in the area. She could not help me.
8. Our dog ran off. It had bitten the postman.
9. They were foreigners. So they had to learn English.
10. I walk to school. I learn ten English words on the way. (2)

6.3 Partizipien nach bestimmten Verben

Partizip nach bestimmten Verben?

Die Verwendung eines ***past participle*** nach Verben der Ruhe (*stand*, *remain*, *lie*) deutet auf Folgen einer vorhergehenden Handlung hin.
Im Deutschen wird oft eine ähnliche Konstruktion verwendet.

› The old car **stood** there **covered** with a sheet.	… **stand** mit einem Laken **zugedeckt** da.
The milk bottle **lay** there **smashed** to pieces.	… **lag zerschmettert** dort.
We **remained seated** when the film had finished.	… **blieben sitzen** …

Die Verwendung eines ***present participle*** nach Verben der Ruhe (*sit*, *stand*, *remain*, *lie*) oder des Kommens und Gehens (*come*, *go*) deutet darauf hin, dass beide Handlungen gleichzeitig erfolgten.
Im Deutschen wird oft das Partizip der Vergangenheit eingesetzt oder zwei Sätze mit *und* verbunden.

› She **came running** up to me.	Sie **kam** auf mich **zugelaufen**.
I can't **stand** here **talking** all day!	… den ganzen Tag hier **stehen** und **schwatzen**.
The cat **sat** there **looking** at me.	… **saß** dort und **sah** mich an.

Auch einige Verben des Zeitverbringens (*spend time*, *waste time*) werden mit dem ***present participle*** verwendet.
Im Deutschen wird hier oft ein ***gerund*** oder ein Nomen (bzw. eine Nominalisierung) benutzt.

› She **spends** hours **cooking**.	… **bringt** Stunden **mit Kochen zu**.
They **wasted** a lot of time **looking for** a parking space.	… **vergeudeten** viel Zeit **beim Parkplatzsuchen**/**auf der Suche nach** …

Einige weitere Ausdrücke (*keep s.o. waiting/standing/working, stop/catch s.o. doing s.th.*) werden mit dem ***present participle*** verwendet.
Im Deutschen steht oft ein Infinitiv.

› My boyfriend kept me waiting.	… ließ mich warten.
Their boss often keeps them working until after 6 p.m.	… lässt sie … arbeiten.
He caught the boys stealing his apples.	… erwischte … beim Äpfelklauen.
The government stopped immigrants entering the country illegally.	… hinderte illegale Einwanderer am Einreisen.

Aufgabe 7

Use the above constructions to make one sentence out of each of the following pairs.

1. They stood outside the cinema. They waited for the doors to open.
   They stood outside the cinema waiting for the doors to open.
   or: They stood waiting for the cinema to open.
2. She just sat there. She watched TV.
3. The children went down to the beach. They ran.
4. The police officers just stood there. They waited for orders.
5. The food remained. Nobody had touched it.
6. He spends a lot of time at discos. He is a good dancer.
7. The farmer caught two campers. They camped in his field without permission.
8. They have wasted a lot of time. They play football at the weekends.
9. The sailor lay on the grass. He was asleep.
10. They sunbathed. They spent a lot of time doing it.
11. I can't stand here all day and wait for you!

Partizip oder Infinitiv ohne *to* nach bestimmten Verben

Nach Verben der „sinnlichen Wahrnehmung" (*see*, *hear*, *watch*, *feel*) wird der **Infinitiv ohne *to*** benutzt, wenn die **ganze Handlung** gesehen, gehört, gefühlt – erlebt wird.

Das **Partizip der Gegenwart** wird benutzt, wenn nur **ein Teil der Handlung** beobachtet wird.

› I saw a strange man **standing** outside the house. Then I saw him **climb** in through the open window.

We watched the Queen **arrive**. For a while we watched the other guests **arriving** but went home before the last guests came.

I heard the front door **open**. Then I heard someone **walking** slowly up the stairs towards my bedroom …

For a second they felt the earth **move**. Then, just as suddenly, the earthquake was over. But they could still feel themselves **shaking** with fear.

Aufgabe 8

Look at the picture and use the switchboard to make ten sentences. Use each verb twice.

When I was in London last week, …

			driv/e(ing) up and down.
		the hot sun	speak(ing) German.
	saw	several people	wait(ing) …
	watched	a police car	tak/e(ing) off.
… I	listened to	a plane	go(ing) to an emergency.
	heard	the traffic	warm(ing) the back of my neck.
	felt	a street musician	look(ing) in the shop windows.
		a hand	play(ing) near the Underground.
			touch(ing) my shoulder. It was …

… my good friend Bob, who had walked up behind me in the street.

6.4 Gerundium und Infinitiv

Das *gerund*

Das ***gerund*** kann verwendet werden

- als (erweitertes) Subjekt oder (erweitertes) Objekt eines Satzes.
  › Skiing is fun. I love skiing.
  Climbing mountains is expensive. I prefer climbing with my friends.

- nach Präpositionen.
  › We are looking forward to visiting London again.
  He paid for his holiday by selling his motorbike.
  Are you used to sleeping with the window open?
  His teacher accused him of cheating in his exams.
  He was fined for driving too fast.

- für kurze Verbote (aber ohne eigenes Objekt).
  › No smoking in the cinema.
  No cycling. **but**: Do not leave bicycles in front of the shop.

- nach bestimmten Verben und Redewendungen.
  › Do you feel like going swimming?
  I love/enjoy/hate/detest learning English.
  We kept on working and put off taking a break until we had finished.
  Would you mind closing the window?

- mit eigenem Sinnsubjekt nach bestimmten Verben.
  › My mum loves listening to pop music but she hates me listening to loud music in bed late at night.
  I'm sick of him playing that awful music!
  Would you mind me opening the window for a minute?

In der formalen Sprache wird die Form mit Possessivbegleiter bevorzugt.
› She said she was tired of his playing loud music at night.
Would you mind my opening the window for a minute?

Hier findest du eine Auflistung der **wichtigsten Verben und Ausdrücke**, die mit dem *gerund* – häufig mit eigenem Sinnsubjekt – verwendet werden.

avoid, deny, can't stand (= kann nicht ausstehen), *can't help* (= kann nicht umhin, …), *enjoy, excuse, forgive, imagine, involve, it's no use/good* (= hat keinen Zweck, …), *it's* (*not*) *worth* (= es lohnt sich (nicht), …), *miss, postpone* (= put off), *prevent, resist, risk, stop, suggest*

Gerund oder Infinitiv nach bestimmten Verben in unterschiedlicher Bedeutung

	mit *gerund*	**mit Infinitiv**
go	We often **go swimming** (shopping, skiing, …). *Wir gehen oft schwimmen …*	We often **go** to our local cinema **to see** a good film. *Wir gehen oft …, um … zu sehen.*
go on	He **went on talking** about himself. *Er redete unentwegt über sich. (= hörte nicht auf)*	He **went on to talk** about his car. *Er erzählte anschließend von seinem Auto. (Themenwechsel)*
regret	I **regret telling** him about my discovery. *Ich bedaure, ihn über meine Entdeckung informiert zu haben. (DAMALS gesagt, JETZT bedauert)*	I **regret to tell** you that the train is over an hour late. *Es tut mir leid, Ihnen (jetzt) sagen zu müssen, … . (schlechte Nachricht kommt jetzt …)*
remember	I **remember going** home. *Ich erinnere mich, dass ich nach Hause ging.*	I **remembered to go** home. *Ich dachte daran, nach Hause zu gehen.*
stop	She **stopped talking**. *Sie hörte auf zu reden.*	She **stopped to talk**. *Sie hielt an, um zu reden.*

Aufgabe 9

Read the email and list the "ing"-forms in the following three categories.

Gerund	Present participle	Progressive form
I like living …	*a living museum*	*I've been living …*

Dear Uncle Jack,

I've been living in Central London for almost a month now and I must say that I like living in the big city. London is a living museum! Sitting on the upper deck of a bus on my way to school the other day I could see over the high wooden fence surrounding a big building site. As well as building workers I could see students looking for Roman remains on the site. Working as an archaeologist must be fun. I wouldn't mind studying archaeology when I leave school.

I love walking around the streets of London after dark. The mist rising from the lakes in the parks is amazing. The atmosphere in the oldest streets which you can only reach by walking through narrow alleys and passageways … I never thought I would find myself writing about a big city like this. But after living in London for nearly four weeks I have got used to hearing the sound of traffic travelling through the city all day and most of the night. Waking up at night, I sometimes wish it were a bit quieter, but living near the centre of a city makes life so much more interesting, don't you think?

I must stop writing now and start doing my homework. I look forward to seeing you at Christmas.

Yours,
Helena

Die Schwierigkeit bei der richtigen Verwendung des englischen *gerund* liegt darin, dass im Deutschen meist eine andere Konstruktion (oft ein Infinitiv) benutzt wird, so dass man nicht daran denkt, das *gerund* zu gebrauchen. Deshalb gehen wir in Aufgabe 10 vom Deutschen aus. Alle Redewendungen, die du brauchst, findest du auf Seite 100.

Aufgabe 10

Translate the following sentences into English. Use gerund constructions.

1. Schwimmen ist eines meiner Hobbies.

2. Ich schwimme gern im Meer.

3. Ich gewöhnte mich bald daran, in Salzwasser zu schwimmen.

4. Im Schwimmbad schwimmen ist nicht so schön.

5. Ich habe nichts dagegen, am Wochenende ins Freibad zu gehen.

6. Mein Bruder hat nichts dagegen, wenn ich ohne ihn gehe.

7. Alte Schallplatten sammeln ist sein Lieblingshobby.

8. Er finanziert sein Hobby dadurch, dass er Zeitungen austrägt.

9. Meine Mutter mag es nicht, wenn er die Zeitungen bei schlechtem Wetter austragen muss.

10. Sie freut sich darauf, dass er bald einen richtigen Job anfängt.

Aufgabe 11

Put in the right form (*gerund* or *infinitive*) of the verb in brackets. Make sure you understand the context before you make your choice.

1.	**(remember – live)**	I was born in London. Sometimes I try … what … in the big city was like but I don't remember much about my early life.
2.	**(move)**	I only remember my family … to the small village where we live now.
3.	**(ask)**	Last week our class went on a school trip to London. Before we left I remembered … my mother for our old address.
4.	**(shop)**	I had a couple of hours to spare while the others went … in Oxford Street.
5.	**(find)**	So I took the Underground to the Elephant and Castle. But I had trouble … 13 Weston Street. The house numbers ran from 1 to 11 and began again at 15. There was a small playground where house number 13 had been.
6.	**(ask)**	I tried … some kids in the playground, but they had not lived there very long.
7.	**(talk)**	Then I asked two women who had stopped … in the street. "Number 13?" said one. "They say 13 is an unlucky number, don't they? The house was empty for years after the last family left."
8.	**(talk – tell)**	She stopped … for a moment while two small children walked past. Then she went on … me about the house. Things my parents had never told me.
9.	**(leave)**	Now I realize why they never regretted … 13 Weston Street, London SE1. Three people had been killed there in the 1960s.
10.	**(live)**	"Nobody wanted … there for a long time afterwards. In the end they pulled the house down. They say it was haunted."
11.	**(mention)**	She went on … various other changes in the area.
12.	**(say)**	She talked for so long that I regret … I lied to her. I said I was in a hurry to catch a train. I had heard enough.

Abschlusstest online 6

Super! Du hast das **Kapitel 6 – Partizipien – Gerundium – Infinitiv** durchgearbeitet. Du weißt, welche Partizipien du verwenden musst, um Relativsätze zu verkürzen und, nach welchen Wortarten das *gerund* zu gebrauchen ist. Außerdem weißt du, dass sich die Bedeutung von Verben je nach Verwendung mit *gerund* oder *infinitive* verändern kann.

So funktioniert der Abschlusstest online:
Um deinen Lernerfolg zu überprüfen, kannst du nun die Tests online machen. Gehe auf
www.klasse5bis10.klett-lerntraining.de/5X7F
und registriere dich wie vorne im Buch beschrieben.

Welche Tests es gibt, siehst du unten in der Tabelle. Nach jedem Test bekommst du eine Auswertung.

Willst du immer im Blick haben, welche Themen du schon kannst oder was du besser nochmal wiederholen solltest? Dann notiere deine Ergebnisse aus den Abschlusstests in der Tabelle.

Mein Ergebnis im Abschlusstest – Kapitel 6

Thema	Mein Ergebnis
Partizipien	
Gerundium – Infinitiv	

7 Das Passiv

7.1 *Simple forms* im Passiv

Du verwendest das Passiv, wenn

- der Täter unbekannt oder so gut wie unbekannt ist.
  › Someone **has eaten** all the food. = All the food **has been eaten**.
- das Objekt des Aktivsatzes wichtiger als der Täter ist.
  › They **made** a big decision. = A big decision **was made**.
- der Täter sogar verheimlicht werden soll.
  › My boss **has** just **made** a terrible mistake!
  = A terrible mistake **has been made**.
- Anweisungen durch Befehle, Schilder usw. gegeben werden.
  Vergleiche:
  › PE Teacher: "You **must** not **wear** street shoes in the gym."
  Notice on door: Street shoes **must** not **be worn** in the gym.

Die einzelnen Formen des Passivs werden im Deutschen mit „werden", im Englischen dagegen mit *to be* gebildet. Du musst also zwischen einer Passivform und der identischen Konstruktion *to be* + Adjektiv unterscheiden (z.B. *I **was** pleased*).

Vergleiche:

I **was** surprised to see her.	I **was surprised** by the rain.
*Ich **war** überrascht, sie zu sehen.*	*Ich **wurde** vom Regen **überrascht**.*

Und so sehen die entsprechenden Formen aus:

	Active	**Passive**
Simple present:	I **write** the emails but	the bills **are written** by my wife.
Simple past:	She **saw** me in town	but John **wasn't seen** by anyone.
Present perfect:	We **haven't sold** our car.	It **has been stolen**.
Past perfect:	They **had gone** and	all the food **had been eaten** when we arrived.

Will-future:	Someone **will drive** you home.	You **will be driven** home.
Auxiliaries:	You **can trust** him but	his friend **can't be trusted**.
	You **shouldn't eat** raw meat	and all water **should be boiled**.
	Someone **may have written**	or he **may have been called**.
Infinitive:	I want **to take** the dog out.	He doesn't need **to be taken** out again tonight.

Aktivsätze ohne Objekt können nicht in Passivsätze „verwandelt" werden, weil das Wichtigste fehlt: ein Objekt, das zum Subjekt des neuen Passivsatzes werden kann. Der Satz *"She fell down."* z. B. muss so bleiben.

Aufgabe 1

You are going on holiday to Malta, but this is your first holiday on your own and you are not always sure what you should do. But the people you ask are very helpful.

On the plane to Malta:

1. *You:* Must I show my passport?
   Friend: Yes, all passports *must be shown*.
2. *You:* Will someone meet us at the airport?
   Friend: Yes, I expect …
3. *You:* And must we open our luggage?
   Friend: Well, usually one or two pieces of luggage … But it's only a formality.
4. *You:* Did your friend Mike book hotel rooms for us?
   Friend: Of course! Our … weeks ago!

At the airport:

5. *You:* What about our luggage? It's quite heavy. Can someone take it to the hotel?
   Friend: That's no problem. Your luggage … to the hotel, but I can carry mine.

In a souvenir shop:

6. *You:* Do the people on Malta make these souvenirs?
   Shop assistant: Oh yes, all our souvenirs …

→

7. *You:* What about these stones? Did you pick them up on the beach?
   Shop assistant: No they … in one of the caves.
8. *You:* Caves?
   Shop assistant: Yes. Malta is famous for its caves.
   You: Do many tourists visit them?
   Shop assistant: Oh yes. The caves … by thousands of tourists every year. Your hotel can arrange a visit.

At the hotel:

9. *You:* When can we take a coach trip round the island?
   Manager: … on any morning of the week.
10. *You:* May we book two seats on this morning's coach?
    Manager: I'm sorry, but seats … (not) … in advance. Just wait outside the hotel. The coach won't be too full.
11. *You:* Have you arranged a trip to the caves for us?
    Manager: Yes. A trip … for Thursday.

Aufgabe 2

You are on holiday in Kenya with a friend. Your friend does not like the hotel – or the country – very much. In the following sentences you have to tactfully contradict what he/she says.

1. Yesterday someone **stole** my shoes. – *I'm sure they weren't stolen.* I expect they wanted to polish them for you! Why don't you ask the manager?
2. Nobody **understands** English in this hotel! – That's not true. English … by most of the people here.
3. I mean nobody in this country **speaks** real English! – So where …?
4. In London, of course! People here **dislike** tourists. – I don't think … here more than in other countries.
5. And they're all thieves! Pickpockets **stole** my friend's wallet here last year. – Well, my wallet … in London last year. –
6. And another thing. **Has** anyone **cleaned** your room yet? – Of course. My room … every day so far. The maid comes in the morning.
7. After she **had made** my bed she asked me – in perfect English – if I would like her to clean the room. – Hmm. When I told her that my bed … n't … since I arrived, she pretended she couldn't speak English.
8. That's strange! Maybe she just **doesn't like** you! – Perhaps you're right. I don't think … by the people here!

Aufgabe 3

Sometimes people wish to divert attention from themselves. Look at the following police report about a peace demonstration in London. Who did these terrible things? In some cases, demonstrators, in other cases – nobody! Or at least that is what you might think when reading this report! Rewrite the report from the point of view of PEACE NOW magazine. Put the verbs in bold type into their active forms and put the real agents back into the sentences. Replace sentences where the agents are in bold type with passive sentences that hide their identities.

Yesterday a forbidden demonstration in Trafalgar Square **was broken up**. A number of people **were arrested** when **violent demonstrators** injured several police officers. After **innocent bystanders** had called the police, about twenty police officers **were brought** to Trafalgar Square. The leader of the demonstration, the well-known troublemaker Jessica Davies, **was requested** to ask her fellow-demonstrators to go home, but she refused. **One or two demonstrators** were taken to Marlborough Street police station. Because they refused to give their names, they **were kept** there overnight. We **have not yet released** the ringleader of the worst demonstration for several years. During the past few months four forbidden demonstrations **have been held**.

Write your article like this, and leave out negative words like "violent, forbidden", etc.

1. A heavily-armed police riot squad … a peaceful demonstration …
2. Angry police officers …
3. After the riot squad …, probably by unnamed police informers,
4. armour-plated police vehicles …
5. Bullying police officers ordered Jessica Davies, the leader of the demonstration, …
6. Angry police armed with heavy sticks …
7. Catherine Binyon, chairperson of PEACE NOW, …
8. During the past few months our peaceful organization …

7.2 *Progressive forms* im Passiv

Es gibt im Passiv nur zwei gängige Verlaufsformen.

Active	**Passive**
Simple present progressive: They **are interviewing** him.	He **is being interviewed** right now.
Simple past progressive: They **were filming** the demonstration when we arrived.	The demonstration **was being filmed** when we arrived.

Aufgabe 4

Say what is – or is not – happening. You will need the progressive forms of the verbs above the pictures. The other words will help you.

1 industrial waste – to discharge

2 rubbish – to dump

3 private cars – not used efficiently

4 valuable raw materials – throw away

5 public transport – not used enough

6 to build

7 to close

8 gas-guzzlers* – to develop

9 not recycled

10 cigarette advertising – not banned

* Benzinschlucker

Aufgabe 5

A member of the Green Party is worried a bout pollution in his constituency[1]. He gives a short speech in Parliament, blaming the Government for many of the problems. A conservative newspaper reports his speech, but does not wish to mention the (Conservative) Government in its report. How would the reporter avoid mentioning the Government – or anybody else? Read the speech and write the report. You do not need to make the changes which are normally required for indirect speech.

"The present Government is doing nothing about air pollution. They are building two new by-passes[2] and another twenty miles of motorway in my constituency alone! Last year they promised to halt construction of a nuclear power station which they were planning, but they have done nothing, and a Government-sponsored company is already surveying[3] land near the River Don in preparation for construction of this power station which nobody wants! Big companies are still polluting the rivers in this beautiful part of Great Britain. Last year big companies were still expanding chemicals factories even though the Government had promised an enquiry into chemical pollution!"

[1] Wahlkreis

[2] Umgehungsstraße

[3] vermessen

7.3 Die Ergänzung durch *by/with*

Ergänzung durch *by/with/of*

Da das Passiv eingesetzt wird, wenn der eigentliche Täter unwichtig, unbekannt, selbstverständlich ist oder verschwiegen werden soll, ist eine Ergänzung des Passivsatzes mit *by* + Täter nur dann sinnvoll, wenn es sich

- um eine Änderung der Gewichtung Subjekt/Objekt handelt, keines von beiden aber so unwichtig ist, dass es ausgelassen werden darf.
  › **Many people** have welcomed the decision. (= not just me)
  The decision has been welcomed by most people.
  John Lennon wrote that song. (= not Paul McCartney)
  That song was written by John Lennon. (= not this song)
- um das Ergebnis einer schöpferischen Arbeit handelt. Der „Schöpfer" sollte erwähnt werden.
  › The picture in the living room was painted **by Picasso**.
  This music was written **by a German pop singer**.

Ohne die Ergänzung wären die Sätze unsinnig. Alle Musikstücke werden geschrieben, alle Gemälde wurden von jemandem gemalt.
Wenn wir nicht wissen wollen, von wem das Lied geschrieben wurde, muss man solche Sätze wenigstens mit einer Orts-, Zeitangabe usw. ergänzen.

› That photo was taken **in France during our last holiday**.
John's glasses were broken **in the playground yesterday**.

Wenn es sich nicht um einen Täter, sondern um ein Material usw. handelt, wird nicht *by*, sondern eine andere Präposition benutzt.

› The house was filled **with smoke**.
The house was built **of stone**.

Aufgabe 6

Make ten sentences from the switchboard using *by, with, of … as* necessary. Use at least four progressive forms.

1. This book 2. Thatched houses 3. Live music 4. Good sandwiches 5. Excellent fruit 6. Gas-guzzlers 7. The environment 8. Young people 9. Many souvenirs 10. Spanish	is/are (not) was/were (not) is/are (not) being was/were (not) being	spoken built polluted played made grown written trained banned sold	in … in Britain. of … with … by … on … as doctors. from … every year.

Aufgabe 7

Be an editor. These are the headlines to twelve news stories which reporters working for your newspaper have written. But no matter what you think about these problems, try to be objective. You have to save space too! So only add *by* … if necessary.

Perhaps you can find another way of expressing the agent if you need one (sentence 10).

1. People are dumping more industrial waste in our rivers than ever before
2. 10 photographers were following Prince William yesterday
3. The Nobel Committee has awarded the peace prize to a dog!
4. Fifth husband is divorcing famous film star
5. Teacher has been "selling" good marks to pupils for years
6. African dictator was spending foreign aid money on arms
7. Champion runner took drugs
8. 3 metres of snow are stopping traffic in northern Scotland
9. Hunters have been killing baby seals again
10. Pop star Rihanna will cancel next concert
11. Man bites dog
12. Heavy rain is flooding many parts of Britain

7.4 Passivsätze mit Verb + Präposition

In Passivsätzen mit Verben, die mit Präposition + Objekt verwendet werden, steht die Präposition immer gleich hinter dem Verb.

Active	Passive
They throw the coke cans **away** when they have finished **with** them.	The coke cans are **thrown away** when they are **finished with**.
He is looking **into** the matter.	The matter is being **looked into**.
We must write **to** them at once.	They must be **written to** at once.
You should look new words **up**.	New words should be **looked up**.

Fragen zum Täter müssen durch *by* ergänzt werden.

Who wrote this book?	Who was this book **written by**?

Aufgabe 8

One of the members of Duddington Rural District Council[1] is a member of the Green Party. At a council meeting last week he spoke about various problems. Other members of the council protested. What did they say? Be careful! You may need to change the tense in some cases.

[1] *Gemeinderat*

1. The council is doing nothing about pollution!

   – That's wrong! Plenty ____________________!

2. I disagree! Nobody is looking into the problem of recycling!

   – Rubbish! The problem ____________________ at this very moment!

   An excellent local firm is already working on a new recycling concept.

3. I don't care what ____________________ by your cousin's firm! We need action *now*! And what about road safety? When are we going to set up a traffic-free zone in the village?

4. I think I can answer that. A traffic-free zone __________ as soon as we have enough money. And it's not just cars and lorries, Jonathan! Mrs Smith was knocked down by one of your Greens on a *bicycle* last week!

5. But she wasn't badly injured. More people ________________ and injured by motorists than by cyclists!
6. But cyclists are a danger to pedestrians! If I had *my* way, I'd arrest them and lock them up for a few days!
   – And if I had my way, it's fast drivers like *you* who ________________!
7. Ladies and gentlemen – *please*! Let us move on to the next point: at the last meeting we were talking about bicycles obstructing the High Street.
   – You mean this matter ________ at a meeting where I was not present?
8. I'm sorry, Jonathan. It wasn't on the agenda[2] sent out to all council members. Pauline brought it up. Pauline?
   – Yes, Jon, the matter ________ at the end of the meeting under "other business[3]".
9. There are bikes everywhere in the village now, thanks to you and your cycle shop, Jonathan! They are obstructing the pavements in the village.
   – I think the pavements ________________ by all those cars!
10. So we need a bigger car park.
    – It's not a bigger car park that ________, Paul. It's fewer cars!
11. We should tow away all those bikes! – Don't be ridiculous, Pauline! Bikes can't ________________! You can *wheel* them away!
12. Not if they're chained up to lamp posts! – But bikes have to ________! Otherwise people steal them. Thirty bikes ________ already this year!
    – Ladies and Gentlemen, *please*! It's almost midnight. We must turn our attention to the last point on the agenda: the proposed biological recycling plant on the edge of the village!

[2] *Tagesordnung*

[3] *Sonstiges*

7.5 Passivsätze mit zwei Objekten

1. Bei Verben mit indirektem und direktem Objekt wird meist die Person (indirektes Objekt) zum Subjekt eines Passivsatzes.

   › He promised **his daughter** an ice cream.
   She was promised an ice cream.

   The prime minister promised **the people** free elections.
   The people were promised free elections.

   At first the government refused **me** a visa.
   At first I was refused a visa (by the government).

   The guide gives **each visitor** a brochure.
   Each visitor is given a brochure (by the guide).

   Die wichtigsten Verben mit zwei Objekten sind:
   to allow, to award, to bring, to deny, to give, to hand (= überreichen), *to leave, to offer, to promise, to refuse, to sell, to send, to show, to teach, to tell*

2. Bei den Verben, die das indirekte Objekt immer mit *to* anschließen, kann nur das direkte Objekt zum Subjekt des Passivsatzes werden.

   › They explained the plan **to us** in great detail.
   The plan was explained to us in great detail. (**not**: We were …)

   Has my daughter introduced you **to the vicar**?
   Have you been introduced to the vicar?

   Die wichtigsten Verben bei denen das indirekte Objekt immer mit *to* angeschlossen wird, sind:
   to announce, to deliver, to demonstrate, to describe, to distribute, to explain, to introduce, to propose/suggest (= vorschlagen), *to say*

Aufgabe 9

Make the indirect object the subject of a new sentence (where possible!).

1. Someone brought him a cup of coffee and a cake.
   He *was brought a cup of coffee and a cake.*
2. He handed me the note.
3. She has never offered me a ride in her car!
4. Didn't he send you an invitation to his party?
5. Haven't they taught you to say "please" if you want something?
6. They won't tell you the truth.
7. The Government is denying us our basic rights!
8. My doctor was giving me an injection when the lights went out.
9. The judges are going to award her first prize in the photographic competition.
10. No one has shown me the photos yet.
11. I didn't steal this bike. Someone sold it to me.
12. Her dad promised her a new skateboard for Christmas.
13. My great-grandfather has left me £5,000 in his will (= *Testament*).

Aufgabe 10

These sentences sound better if the direct object becomes the subject. Make any other changes that are necessary.

1. Someone delivered this parcel to the wrong address.
2. I can't explain this problem to people who know nothing about cricket.
3. Nobody has introduced them to the President yet.
4. One can only describe the scenery to you with the help of these photos.
5. I propose the following solution to you.
6. After the chemistry teacher had demonstrated the experiment to his students, the laboratory was full of smoke.
7. An official announced the results of the elections to the angry crowd.
8. No one said anything about this to me.
9. Helpers are distributing clothes to the refugees.
10. Someone suggested an alternative to the worried workers.

7.6 Unpersönliche Sätze und passivähnliche Konstruktionen

1. Wie bei den Verben mit zwei Objekten können unpersönliche Sätze manchmal verbessert – und im Englischen auch verkürzt – werden, wenn eine Person an den Satzanfang gerückt wird.

   Vergleiche die deutsche und englische Version des folgenden Satzes:
   Es wird behauptet, dass er Nudeln mag.
   Von ihm wird (es) behauptet, dass er Nudeln mag.
   It is said that he likes noodles. (*unpersönlich*)
   They say that he likes noodles. (*schon besser!*)
   He is said **to like** noodles. (*die beste Lösung*)

   Im zweiten Satz ist der Täter unbekannt – ein typischer Fall fürs Passiv! Im dritten Satz hast du eine bekannte Person als Subjekt eingesetzt und den schwerfälligen Nebensatz mit *that* durch eine einfache Infinitiv + Objekt-Konstruktion ersetzt.

   Auch wenn ein Nebensatz mit *that* beibehalten werden muss, wird ein Satz mit persönlichem Subjekt vorgezogen.
   › Someone told **us** that the plane was quite safe.
   We were told that **the plane** was quite safe.
   or: The plane **was said** to be quite safe.

   Diese Konstruktion ist nicht auf Lebewesen beschränkt, sondern kann überall eingesetzt werden, wo das Subjekt zu unbestimmt erscheint.
   › People considered that **his plan** was crazy.
   His plan was considered **to be** crazy.

   Die **wichtigsten Verben** mit diesen Konstruktionen sind Verben des Denkens, Fühlens, Behauptens und Vermutens:
   to assume/suppose (= vermuten), *to believe, to claim* (= behaupten), *to consider, to feel, to find* (= herausfinden), *to know, to report, to say, to tell, to think, to understand*

Da es sich um unsichere Behauptungen handelt, wird oft die Verlaufsform des Infinitivs (*to be* + *-ing*) verwendet.

› She was thought **to be living** in France. (= now)

Für Situationen in der Vergangenheit, die zum Zeitpunkt der Behauptung vielleicht nicht mehr zutreffen, brauchst du den *perfect infinitive*.

› She was thought **to have been living** in France before she came to Germany.

2. Verben, die in der Aktivform durch einen Infinitiv ohne *to* ergänzt werden (besonders *see*, *hear*, *make* = lassen) müssen in Passivsätzen durch einen Infinitiv mit *to* ergänzt werden.

› Someone heard him **leave**.	= He was heard **to leave**.
They often make me **wait**.	= I'm often made **to wait**.

Eine Ausnahme ist *let*.

› The terrorists let their hostages **go** at midnight.	The hostages were let **go** at midnight.

Aufgabe 11

After a bank robbery in London, one of the clerks who had been working in the bank when the robbers arrived tells her story. Rewrite what she says as a short newspaper report.

1. Our manager had told us that our bank was robbery-proof.
2. People said that the alarm system was perfect. But the robbers had no trouble getting in.
3. We now feel that the bank's security arrangements were inadequate.
4. It is believed that the robbers had been hiding in the bank all night. They surprised us when we arrived for work.
5. They told us to put up our hands.
6. Then they made us lie down on the floor.
7. The police suppose that the gang is the same one that robbed the National Westminster Bank in Croydon last month.
8. Everybody knows that these men are dangerous criminals!
9. The robbers told us not to move for ten minutes.
10. They said there were other crooks outside, watching in case we gave the alarm.
11. People outside the bank saw the robbers leave in a fast car.
12. When they had gone we found that the manager, Mr Simms, had had a mild heart attack!

Abschlusstest online 7

Toll! Du hast **Kapitel 7 – Das Passiv** durchgearbeitet. Du kannst Sätze im Aktiv und auch im Passiv bilden und hast die Verlaufsformen des Passiv wiederholt. Du weißt nun alles über Passivsätze mit Verben und Objekten und über passivähnliche Konstruktionen.

So funktioniert der Abschlusstest online:
Um deinen Lernerfolg zu überprüfen, kannst du nun die Tests online machen. Gehe auf
www.klasse5bis10.klett-lerntraining.de/5X7F
und registriere dich wie vorne im Buch beschrieben.

Welche Tests es gibt, siehst du unten in der Tabelle. Nach jedem Test bekommst du eine Auswertung.

Willst du immer im Blick haben, welche Themen du schon kannst oder was du besser nochmal wiederholen solltest? Dann notiere deine Ergebnisse aus den Abschlusstests in der Tabelle.

Mein Ergebnis im Abschlusstest – Kapitel 7

Thema	Mein Ergebnis
Das Passiv	

8 Modale Hilfsverben

8.1 Gebrauch und Formen modaler Hilfsverben

Modale Hilfsverben unterscheiden sich von anderen Verben dadurch, dass sie weder eine Handlung beschreiben (*I* ***speak*** *English*), noch – wie andere Hilfsverben – der Bildung einer Zeitform dienen (z.B. *to be/to have* + *-ing/-ed*). Sie drücken eine Modalität in Zusammenhang mit einer Handlung aus.

› I **can speak** English (*can* = Fähigkeit),
we **may go** swimming (*may* = Möglichkeit oder Erlaubnis),
she **must learn** (*must* = Notwendigkeit),
they **should drive** carefully,
he **ought to drive** slowly (*should/ought to* = Verpflichtung).

Formen

Modale Hilfsverben gibt es im Englischen in höchstens zwei Formen, wobei die zweite keineswegs dem ***simple past*** entspricht. Die Lücken füllen wir mit sogenannten „Ersatzverben" (*substitutes*).

Achtung: Es gibt weder eine Grundform zur Bildung der *will*-Zukunft noch Partizipien zur Bildung der Verlaufs- und Perfektformen.

Aufgabe 1

Read the following brochure from the Action Group RETURN IMBER and make three lists. List 1 should contain all the modal auxiliaries in the text. List 2 should contain all the substitutes (Ersatzformen) you can find. Put all the tense-forming auxiliaries in List 3.

Ministry of Defence

EVACUATION ORDER

Defence of the Realm Act – 15th October, 1943

NOTICE is hereby given that the Village of Imber in the County of Wiltshire is to be evacuated on 1st December 1943.

This Evacuation Order must be observed by all residents. Any persons who are not able to find accommodation in the area should apply to the Commanding Officer, Southern Command, Wilton, Wiltshire, who may be able to help.

Residents must take all their furniture and possessions with them, as no one will be allowed to return after the evacuation date.

From 2nd December 1943, all roads across this section of Salisbury Plain will be CLOSED TO THE GENERAL PUBLIC.

This Evacuation is for the duration of the War. Residents will be able to return to their homes as soon as the situation permits.

No exceptions can be made to this Order, which is issued in the interests of National Security

GOD SAVE THE KING!

It is now about 80 years since the last 150 residents of Imber, the most isolated village in southern England, had to leave their homes. They were allowed to take their possessions with them but were forbidden to return to the village even after the war.

The tiny village, of which only St Giles Church, Imber Court and a few half-ruined buildings have been allowed to remain, is situated right in the middle of Salisbury Plain – and in the middle of Army artillery ranges and battle-training areas.

The general public may only visit the village with the Army's permission on a few days every year, and people must not leave the roads to walk across the deserted meadows because they might be injured by unexploded ammunition from tanks and guns.

The action group RETURN IMBER believes that the Army ought to keep its promise and should return Imber to the people!

8.2 *Must* und *can/could*

must

Notwendigkeit		
ich muss	I must	I have to
ich musste	–	I had to
ich habe gemusst	–	I have had to
ich werde müssen	–	I will have to
ich müsste	–	I would have to

Von *must*, das viel dringlicher klingt als *have to*, existiert nur eine Präsensform. Für die anderen Formen benutzt man *have to*.

Have to wird als Vollverb behandelt. Fragen und Verneinungen werden also wie gewohnt mit *do/does* – *did* gebildet.

› **Do** I **have to** eat all of this? – Yes, you **mustn't** leave anything!
Did she **have to** leave so early? Was it really necessary?

In der Umgangssprache findest du aber auch Formen mit *got*.

› **Have** we **got to** do our homework now? = **Do** we **have to** do …?

Beachte, dass „nicht müssen" im Englischen mit *needn't* ausgedrückt wird. *You* ***mustn't****!* ist ein Verbot, *You* ***must*** ein Gebot!

› **Must** we go to the meeting?
– I'm afraid we **must**. But we **needn't** stay long.

can/could

Fähigkeit		
ich kann	I can	I am able to
ich habe gekonnt	–	I have been able to
ich konnte	(I could)	I was able to
ich könnte	I could	I would be able to
ich werde können	–	I will be able to

Es gibt nur die zwei Formen *can* und *could*. ***Could*** kann nur in eindeutigen Kontexten mit klarem Vergangenheitsbezug mit „konnte" gleichgesetzt werden, weil es meist für die **Möglichkeitsform** steht.

Kontext eindeutig:
Could you? = Könnten Sie?
› Could you come quickly, doctor? – Of course. I can come now.

Could you? = Konnten Sie?
› You went to the circus last night? Could you see everything?
– Of course. We were sitting in the front row.

Kontext unklar:
Could you go?
mit Ersatzform: Were you able to go? – No, we weren't.

Aufgabe 2

Put in the right forms of *must*, *have to* or *needn't*.

1. I'm a bit tired this evening. ________ we __________ to go to Marilyn's party, Alan?
2. We ______________ go if you're too tired. I'll ring her and say we can't come.
3. You've had a busy week. You ______________ overdo things.
4. No. I ________ to work very hard today and I __________________ to work even harder next week.
5. Why?
   – Because our department __________________ to move into new offices.
6. We ________________ to move three times in the last five years!
7. Why __________ you __________ to move so many times?
8. It's a long story.
   – OK! You ______________ tell me if it's so long!
9. You're right. I think I really __________ go to bed now.
   – Goodnight, Grandma!

Aufgabe 3

Put in the right form – or a substitute – of the verb used in the first half of the sentence.

1. I can't help you today but I will ______________ help you tomorrow.
2. Why must I help him? He __________ never __________ to help me!
3. Why can't you do your German homework this week?
   You ______________________ do it all right last week.
4. Can you explain the present perfect tense to me? I ____________ never ______________________ to understand when it is used!
5. John and Sarah won't be able to go on holiday until next month, but Claudia and I hope ________________________________ go next week.
6. You'll have to wait. The doctor _______________________________ see two other more serious cases first.
7. Have you been able to go gliding often?
   – Not often, but I want ________________________________ spend more time on my hobby next year.
8. Could you help me?
   – If I had more time I ___________________________ to help you.
9. Why can't he tell you the answer?
   – He said he ________________________________ find the website yet.
10. I haven't been able to go skiing yet because I _________________________ ____________________ find my ski boots.
11. Has he had to leave school?
    – No, but he ____________________________ work harder next year.

8.3 *May/might*

1. Erlaubnis

Darf ich?	May I?	Am I allowed to?
ich durfte	–	I was allowed to
ich habe gedurft	–	I have been allowed to
Ich werde dürfen	–	I will be allowed to
Dürfte ich?	Might I?	–

Die Frageform wird als Bitte um Erlaubnis verwendet. Die bejahte oder verneinte Form wird in der Beantwortung oder im üblichen Sinne von „dürfen" benutzt.

› **May** I/we **watch** TV this evening? – You **may watch** TV until 11 o'clock but you **may not watch** any violent films!

Might wird in höflichen Fragen benutzt und steht für *may* in der indirekten Rede nach dem Einführungsverb in der Vergangenheit.

Die Antwort auf die höfliche Frage *Might we …?* ist niemals *you might*, sondern fast immer das „großzügig" klingende *you may*.

› **Might** I **ask** you a favour? – Of course you **may**!
May John **stay** the night? = He **asked** if John **might** stay the night.

Die Ersatzformen sind im Allgemeinen etwas schwächer im Ausdruck.

› Dad says I **may** stay up later tonight. (*Sondererlaubnis*)
I **am allowed to** stay up until 11 o'clock most nights. (*generell*)

2. Möglichkeit/Vermutung

May und *might* können auch Unterschiede in der Wahrscheinlichkeit ausdrücken. *May* wird in dieser Bedeutung selten als Frage verwendet. In der Verneinung gibt der Kontext Aufschluss, ob es sich um eine Möglichkeit oder die Verweigerung der Erlaubnis handelt.

› He **may not** come.	(= Möglicherweise kommt er nicht.)
She **must** stay in bed.	Sie muss im Bett blieben.
She **may not** get up.	Sie darf nicht aufstehen.

Im Deutschen wird *may* oft mit „können" oder „möglicherweise" übersetzt.

› They **may** come if you invite them.	= **Möglicherweise** kommen sie …
She **might** agree, but I don't think so.	= Sie **könnte vielleicht** einverstanden sein …

Aufgabe 4

Put in the right form – or a substitute – of *may*.

1. He may be a good football player but he won't ______ to play for us again unless he learns to play fair!
2. Might I ask whether I'll ______ stay in Britain?
3. Caroline's mum says she may go to the cinema tonight but she (not) ______ stay out later than 10 o'clock.
4. Please may I go, too, Mum? – No, you ______
5. Why not? Tarik ______ go last week!
6. The weather forecast said that it ______ rain later.
7. I don't know whether we ______ go camping next month.
8. ______ watch TV when you were a boy, Grandad?
9. There was no TV when I was a boy, and we (not) ______ waste time, either!
10. ______ I come in? – Of course.
11. ______ I ask you exactly what your plans are?
12. If she went by plane she ______ arrive in time.
13. If you buy a lottery ticket you ______ win £1,000.
14. So if I bought ten lottery tickets I ______ win £10,000?
15. I ______ as well tell you that I'm too busy to see anyone at the moment.

Aufgabe 5

What would you say in the following situations?

1. A good friend has a book that you would like to borrow.
   "______________________________?"
2. You want to use your friend's dad's computer. You have to be quite polite about it! "______________________________ possibly ______________________________?"
3. You look closely at a £5 note. It looks like a forgery! You show it to your mum. "I think ______________________________"
4. Is your friend too young to watch the horror film with you? Perhaps, but be tactful! "I think ______________________________"
5. A holiday in Spain next year? It's very possible.
   "We ______________________________"
6. A holiday on Hawaii? Less likely!
   "If we had more money ______________________________"
7. Borrow my car? No! "You ______________________________!"
8. Concert in Edinburgh next week? Alone? Your parents won't let you and your friend go. "I don't think we ______________________________"
9. But if your big brother goes with you.
   "If my brother went with us I ______________________________"
10. Abolish school uniform? Yes, your English friend is probably right.
    "You ______________________________"
11. Abolish pocket money? You are not sure this is such a good idea.
    "It ______________________________"
12. You are staying with your grandparents.
    They do not want to let you watch your favourite TV programme.
    You protest: "At home I've always ______________________________!"

8.4 *Shall/should*

Verpflichtung

Soll ich?	Shall I/we?	–
ich sollte	I should	I ought to
Sollten wir?	Should we?	Ought we to?
ich hätte sollen	I should have	I ought to have

Wie bei *may/might* sind die Frageformen relativ eindeutig. Bei verneinten Fragen wird meistens *should* verwendet.

› **Shall** we go into the garden? = Sollen/Wollen wir …?
Should we wait a little longer? = Sollten wir …?
Shouldn't they be here by now? = Sollten sie nicht …?

Bei *ought to* handelt es sich nicht um eine Ersatzform, denn dieses Verb füllt keine Lücken aus. Das Verb *ought to* drückt ebenfalls „sollten" aus.

Ought ist nur ein halbherziges Hilfsverb! Der darauf folgende Infinitiv braucht das *to* (wie bei *to want to*: *"I want to ask you a question"*), während eine Frage (s. oben) durch Umstellung (wie bei einem echten Hilfsverb) gebildet wird.

Für die anderen Bedeutungen von „sollen" gibt es im Englischen entsprechende Übersetzungen. Hier einige Beispiele:

- „sollen" = es wird vermutet, behauptet

Jogging **soll** ungesund sein.	Jogging **is supposed**/**is said** to be unhealthy.
Er **sollte** klug sein.	He **was said**/**supposed** to be clever.
Sie **soll** in London wohnen.	**They say** she lives in London.

- „sollen" = es ist (meist von Dritten) angeordnet

Was **soll** ich tun?	What **shall** I do? (*Bitte um Rat*) What **am** I to do? (*verzweifelte Bitte*) What **am** I **supposed** to do? (*Was erwartest du von mir?*)
Wir **sollen** hier warten.	We **are supposed** to wait here. We **are** to wait here. (*strenger*)
Sie **sollten** entlassen werden.	They **were** to be fired. (*Vorhaben*)
Er sagte, ich **solle** in Zukunft vorsichtiger sein.	He said I **was** to be/**should** be more careful in future. (*indirekte Rede*)

- „sollen" = etwas ist festgelegt, vereinbart, vom Schicksal verfügt worden

Er **sollte** am Montag kommen.	He **was (supposed)** to come on Monday.
Leider **sollte** der Komponist mit 33 Jahren jung sterben.	Unfortunately the composer **was** to die at the early age of 33.

- „sollen" = es wäre vielleicht gut/besser …

Wir **sollten** (lieber nicht) warten.	We**'d (= had) better** not wait.

Aufgabe 6

An English-speaking friend is staying with you. What would you say to him/her in the following situations? Use the correct form of *shall/should*, *ought to* or one of the phrases to translate the German verb *sollen*.

1. Du schlägst eine Radtour aufs Land vor: ________________ a bike ride in the country?
2. Es sieht nach Regen aus. Perhaps we ________________ coats with us.
3. Trotzdem wäre es nicht gut, zu weit weg zu fahren.
   Perhaps we ________________ too far.
4. Der kleine See am Waldesrand soll zum Baden gut sein.
   The little lake on the edge of the forest ________________.
5. Ihr radelt los. Warne deinen Freund/deine Freundin davor, auf der linken Straßenseite zu fahren. Hey! You ________________ cycle on the left-hand side!
6. You're right! I ________________ to know that by now!
7. Ihr kommt am See an. Nach dem Baden zeigst du deinem Freund/deiner Freundin ein altes verfallenes Haus. Darin soll es spuken!
   See that old house over there? ________________ to be haunted.
8. Haunted? ________________ have a look around?
9. Gute Idee! Aber die Tür ist verschlossen, und da hängt ein Schild: ZUTRITT VERBOTEN! That sign means nobody ________________ to go inside.
10. Perhaps we ________________ go in, then.
11. Ja: Wenn uns jemand sehen sollte, gäb's vielleicht Ärger.
    Yes, if ________________ we might get into trouble.
12. Jetzt ist's eigentlich Zeit, nach Hause zu fahren.
    I think we ________________ go home before it gets dark.

8.5 *Will/would*

1. **Bereitschaft**, **Wollen** (oft ohne Hilfsverb im Deutschen)

› I'**ll talk** to Dad about it.	Ich **spreche** mit …
I've asked him to come but he **won't**.	… er **will** nicht.
Will you please be quiet!	**Wollen** Sie bitte …!
If you **will**, just wait a moment …	Wenn Sie sich … gedulden **wollen**.

2. **Gewohnheit**

Will/would werden oft benutzt, um gegenwärtige oder ehemalige Gewohnheitshandlungen auszudrücken. Im Deutschen wird die Gewohnheitsmäßigkeit mit anderen Mitteln ausgedrückt.

› Many London commuters **will** travel over 50 miles to work every day.	Viele Pendler fahren **regelmäßig** …
She **would** sit there for hours watching TV.	Sie **pflegte** stundenlang fernzusehen.
He **would** never listen to a word I said.	**Gewöhnlich wollte** er mir nie zuhören.

Ist die Gewohnheit lästig oder ärgerlich, wird das Hilfsverb (ähnlich wie bei *do/does* – *did* in Aussagesätzen) stark betont.

› He ***will*** stay up late!	Er bleibt **doch immer** so lange auf!
She ***won't*** do as she's told!	Sie hört **nie** auf mich!
I ***did*** warn them, but they ***would*** try the food!	Ich warnte sie, aber sie **mussten/bestanden darauf** …
Boys ***will*** be boys!	Jungen sind **nun mal** so. (Sprichwort) = machen immer wieder dieselben Dummheiten!

Im Gegensatz zum „Gewohnheitsverb" *used to*, drückt *will/would* den „Willen" verstärkt aus. *Used to* ist neutraler.

› I **used to** walk three miles to school each morning. (= *Gewohnheit*)
He **would** walk three miles to school in order to save his bus fare.
(= *gewollte Sparmaßnahme in der Vergangenheit*)

Als Übersetzung für das deutsche Verb „wollen" kommen außerdem folgende Wörter in Frage:

- *to want to* (Allzweckverb)
  › He **wants to** come with us. — Er **will** mit uns mitkommen.
- *to wish to* (stilistisch vornehmer)
  › Judge: "**Do** you **wish to** say anything in your defence?" — Richter: „**Möchten** Sie irgendetwas zu Ihrer Verteidigung sagen?"
- *to desire to* (noch vornehmer als *wish*)
  › The Queen **desires to** speak to you. — Die Königin **wünscht**, Sie zu sprechen.
- *to be willing to* = bereit sein, gerne wollen
  › **Are** you **willing to** listen? — **Willst** du mir zuhören?
  I'**m** quite **willing to** stay here. — Ich **will gerne** hier bleiben.
- *to intend to*, *to mean to* = vorhaben, *to be going to* = die Absicht haben
  › The police officer asked her how long she **intended to** stay. — Der Polizist fragte sie, wie lange sie bleiben **wollte**.
  I **meant to** ask her but I forgot. — Ich **wollte** sie fragen …
  He **is going to** get married. — Er **will** heiraten.
- *would like to* = möchten
  › What **would** you **like** to do? — Was **willst**/**möchtest** du machen?
  I'**d like** to watch a film. — Ich **will**/**möchte** mir einen Film ansehen.

Aufgabe 7

How would you translate these sentences? Don't just use *want* all the time. Pick the most suitable verb.

1. Wollen Sie mit mir sprechen, Mr Richards?

   ____

2. Ach, Jana! Ja. Ich wollte dich heute Vormittag anrufen!

   ____

3. Ich wollte dich fragen, ob du am Klassenausflug teilnehmen willst (= möchtest).

   ____

   ____

4. Ich wollte eigentlich (= really) am Wochenende zu Hause bleiben.

   ____

5. Meine Tante will uns besuchen.

   ____

6. Sie wollten (= hatten die Absicht) den Film sehen, wollten aber nicht wegen Karten anstehen.

   ____

   ____

7. Was wollen (= vorhaben) Sie mit dem Geld tun?

   ____

8. Ich will (= Planung) ein Mountainbike kaufen.

   ____

9. Ein Mountainbike habe ich immer haben wollen.

   ____

Abschlusstest online 8

Gut gemacht! Du hast **Kapitel 8 – Modale Hilfsverben** durchgearbeitet. Du hast alle Hilfsverben wiederholt, die du bei Fragen oder Wahrscheinlichkeiten benutzen kannst. *Will* und *would*, *mustn't* und *should* kannst du richtig verwenden.

So funktioniert der Abschlusstest online:
Um deinen Lernerfolg zu überprüfen, kannst du nun die Tests online machen. Gehe auf
www.klasse5bis10.klett-lerntraining.de/5X7F
und registriere dich wie vorne im Buch beschrieben.

Welche Tests es gibt, siehst du unten in der Tabelle. Nach jedem Test bekommst du eine Auswertung.

Willst du immer im Blick haben, welche Themen du schon kannst oder was du besser nochmal wiederholen solltest? Dann notiere deine Ergebnisse aus den Abschlusstests in der Tabelle.

Mein Ergebnis im Abschlusstest – Kapitel 8

Thema	Mein Ergebnis
Modale Hilfsverben	

9 Relativsätze

9.1 Notwendige und nicht-notwendige Relativsätze

Notwendige Relativsätze

Der notwendige Relativsatz (***defining relative clause***) vermittelt notwendige Informationen über eine Person oder eine Sache im Hauptsatz. Ohne diese Informationen wäre die Person oder die Sache nicht identifizierbar.
Vergleiche:

› **Angela Barnes** sits next to me in my class.	(Die Person ist namentlich genannt und somit deutlich identifiziert.)
The girl sits next to me in my class.	(Es fehlt eine eindeutige Identifikation des Mädchens. Der Satz ist verwirrend, unklar.)
The girl who sits next to me is Angela Barnes.	(Mit dem *who*-Nebensatz ist das Mädchen eindeutig identifiziert.)

Du musst dir also abgewöhnen, immer zwischen Haupt- und Nebensatz ein Komma setzen.

Ein notwendiger Relativsatz bildet eine Einheit mit dem Begriff, den er beschreibt, und wird im Englischen ohne Pause d.h. ohne Kommas angehängt, denn im Englischen ist das Komma immer ein „Pausenzeichen".

Nicht-notwendige Relativsätze

Der „nicht bestimmende" Relativsatz (***non-defining relative clause***) gibt **zusätzliche Informationen** über eine Person oder eine Sache wieder, die nicht zur Identifikation der Person oder Sache notwendig sind.
Vergleiche:

› **The girl who lives next door** is a good friend of mine.	(wird ohne Pause gesprochen)
That girl, who lives next door, is a good friend of mine.	(wird mit kurzen Pausen bei den Kommas gesprochen)

Es genügt ein Wörtchen wie *that*, im Gegensatz zu *the*, um eine Person deutlich zu identifizieren. Die Kommas funktionieren wie Klammern, zwischen denen in der Schriftsprache oft zusätzliche Informationen stehen.

Wenn wir die Kommas durch Klammern ersetzen, sehen die beiden Relativsatztypen so aus:

› The old man who lives next door will be 93 next week.
John Wilkins (who lives next door) will be 93 next week.

In dieser Form ist die Funktion des Relativsatzes in beiden Sätzen klar.

Aufgabe 1

In each situation use *person, tool, device, thing* etc. to define the following things.

*Denke daran, dass zwischen Haupt- und Nebensatz bei notwendigen Relativsätzen **kein** Komma steht.*

1. A mobile is a telephone *which/that you can carry in your pocket*.
2. A toaster is a device ________________.
3. A winner is a ________________.
4. Dinner is a meal ________________.
5. A fridge is ________________.
6. A bike is ________________.
7. A manager is ________________.
8. A watch is ________________.
9. Soap is ________________.
10. Jam is ________________.
11. Commas are ________________.

Aufgabe 2

Let's see if you know the difference between defining and non-defining relative clauses.
Complete the sentences with suitable parts from the switchboard.
Sometimes you need a defining relative clause and sometimes a non-defining relative clause.

...	,	who which that	teaches us is 16 years old were very expensive is in the garage had red hair	,	...

1. I saw the Harry Potter films first. Then Mum bought me all the books
   ____.
2. He only bought cheap paperbacks. He didn't buy books ______________
   ____.
3. I have two sisters. This is a photo of my sister ______________
   ____.
4. My friend Harry _______________________________
   ______________________________ lives in Bournemouth.
5. The woman ______________________________ French is OK.
6. Mr Strickland _______________________________
   German is very strict.
7. Mum drives the car ______________________________.
8. My dad uses his old bike ______________________________ too.
9. My girlfriend ______________________________ lives next door to me.
10. There's a girl ______________________________ in my class at school.

9.2 Die Relativpronomen als Subjekt und Objekt: *who/which/that*

Pronomen als Subjekt des Relativsatzes

Diese Relativpronomen können als Subjekt im Satz verwendet werden.

Notwendiger Relativsatz
who/that für Personen/Lebewesen:
The man **who/that** took the photo is my uncle.

which/that für Dinge:
The car **which/that** my mother drives is brand new.

Nicht-notwendiger Relativsatz
who für Personen/Lebewesen:
Doug Smith, **who** took the photo, is a friend of mine.

which für Dinge:
That old car, **which** my father drives, is nearly 20 years old.

Das Relativpronomen *that* darf hier nicht verwendet werden.

Pronomen als Objekt des Relativsatzes

Hier gelten die gleichen Regeln wie für das Subjekt – nur, dass in der Schrift- bzw. gehobenen Sprache der Objektfall *whom* bei Personen benutzt wird.

Notwendiger Relativsatz
The man **who(m)/that** I saw was very tall.

The girl **who(m)/that** I was talking to is only 15.

Nicht-notwendiger Relativsatz
The robber, **who(m)** I only saw for a few seconds, was very tall.

Jennifer Jones, **who(m)** I was talking to when you arrived, is 15.

Ist das Relativpronomen Objekt im Relativsatz, kann es – **nur** beim **notwendigen** Relativsatz – sogar weggelassen werden (***contact clause***).

› The man I saw was very tall.
The girl I was talking to is only 15.

Nur in der gehobenen Schriftsprache findet man die im Deutschen noch übliche Fügung „Präposition + Relativpronomen".

› The man **to whom** I was talking is 84.
Der Mann, **mit dem** ich sprach, ist 84.

Nach Präpositionen ist die *whom*-Form obligatorisch.
Das Pronomen *that* darf nicht nach Präpositionen benutzt werden.

Viel häufiger – auch in der Schriftsprache – ist die Verbannung der Präposition ans Satzende.
Hier gilt genauso: Ist das Relativpronomen **Objekt** im **notwendigen** Relativsatz, kann es weggelassen werden (***contact clause***). Diese Konstruktion wird in der gesprochenen Umgangssprache bevorzugt.

gehobene Schriftsprache:	The man **to whom** I was talking is 84.
normale Sprache:	The man **who** I was talking **to** is 84.
Umgangssprache:	The man I was talking **to** is 84.

Achtung:
Das Pronomen darf weggelassen werden, nicht aber die Präposition!

Aufgabe 3

Connect the two sentences with a suitable relative pronoun. You can sometimes, as in sentence 1, leave out the object pronoun in the *contact clause*.

1. Have you finished the book? I lent you it last month!
   Have you finished the book which/that I lent you last month?
   oder: Have you finished the book I lent you last month?
2. Have you played the new game? I lent it to your sister Caroline.
3. This is the boy. I saw him at the party last week.
4. Here's my new bike. I got it for my birthday.
5. This is Linda. We talked to her at Jim's party.
6. They are the new group. You heard them on the internet yesterday.
7. John didn't see the car. The robbers escaped in it.
8. We all know Mickey Mouse. Walt Disney invented him.
9. I like milk chocolate. You can buy it all over the world.
10. Have you read Petra's email? She sent it two days ago.
11. You're the man. I've been waiting for you since lunchtime.
12. Here is my bike. I left it in the garden overnight.
13. He wrote to a Scottish girl. He met her in Spain last month.

Aufgabe 4

Write the correct relative pronouns (*who*/*which*/*that*) in the gaps. You also have to insert a few commas (only a few)! Also try and leave out the relative pronoun where possible.

Rugby is a game ______ is extremely popular in Britain, France, Australia, South Africa, New Zealand and in fact many other Commonwealth countries in ______ there is the British way of life. The game was 'invented' by a boy ______ was a pupil at Rugby School in 1823. He was the first player ______, during a normal game of football, in ______ players normally only kicked the ball, picked up the ball, ______ in those days was not perfectly round but slightly oval, as it still is in Rugby and American football today and ran with it.
There are two types of Rugby: Rugby Union ______ is an amateur sport played at schools, and Rugby League, a professional sport ______ many people watch every Saturday in the North of England.
There are fifteen players in a Rugby Union team and only thirteen in a Rugby League team. International Rugby matches ______ the French and Welsh enjoy more than soccer matches are played under Rugby Union rules and are well attended by thousands of fans ______ often travel long distances to see the games.
The 'inventor' of the game, William Webb Ellis ______ few people know by name became a clergyman* in later life and died in 1872.
Rugby is also a game ______ women enjoy playing. Most men's teams also have a women's team ______ play most Saturdays.

* Geistlicher

9.3 Das Relativpronomen im Genitivfall: *whose/of which*

Neben den Relativpronomen „der/die/das" usw. als Subjekt und Objektpronomen gibt es natürlich Relativsätze, die im Deutschen mit dem Genitivpronomen „dessen/deren" anfangen.
Im Englischen benutzt man sowohl im notwendigen als auch im nicht-notwendigen Relativsatz das Pronomen *whose* bei Personen und *of which* bei Sachen.
Das Relativpronomen *whose* wird jedoch auch zunehmend in Bezug auf Sachen verwendet, um das nachgestellte, schwerfällige *of which* zu vermeiden.

› Edison was an inventor **whose** ideas changed the world.
Edison war ein Erfinder, **dessen** Ideen die Welt veränderten.

J.K. Rowling, **whose** books almost everybody knows, invented Harry Potter.
J.K. Rowling, **deren** Bücher fast jeder kennt, erfand Harry Potter.

Basque, the origins **of which** are unknown, is spoken in Spain.
Basque, **whose** origins are unknown, is spoken in Spain.
Baskisch, **dessen** Ursprung unbekannt ist, wird in Spanien gesprochen.

Those are the shops the windows **of which** were smashed.
Those are the shops **whose** windows were smashed.
Das sind die Läden, **deren** Fenster eingeschlagen wurden.

Aufgabe 5

Commas are also needed for genetive pronouns in defining and non-defining relative clauses. Let's see if you can use the right pronouns here and put the commas in the right places or leave them out!

Three students meet on the first day at university.

1. One of them is Kevin. His friend Nils has just arrived from Germany.
2. Nils is the German exchange student. His parents invited Kevin to stay during the summer vacation.
3. Kevin's best friend John is standing in front of the noticeboard in the corridor. Its notices are usually very interesting.
4. Kevin introduces his two friends to each other. "This is John. His parents are good friends of ours."
5. "John, this is Nils, my German friend. I stayed with his parents during the summer vacation."
6. "Hello, John. I'm the exchange student from Germany. My room is on the floor above yours."
7. "Pleased to meet you. Is that your car outside? The blue one. Its windows are all open."
8. "Did I leave the windows open? It was so hot in town! I was stuck behind a long line of cars. Their drivers all seemed to be asleep!"
9. "Should I go downstairs and shut the windows? Are there many car thieves on the campus?"
   – "Last term thieves stole several cars. Their owners had forgotten to lock them!"
10. "I'll go down and lock my car right away." But suddenly the three students heard a voice from a loudspeaker in the corridor: "Will the owner of the blue car, German registration number HN-LS 317, please come downstairs at once. Your car's windows are open and the doors are not locked."

Aufgabe 6

These are notes for a newspaper article. Can you join them with *relative clauses* and write the article?

Old country (*ländlich*) railway station – Council (*Gemeinderat*) wanted to pull it down – saved at the last minute. The "Save our Station" campaign – leader Robin Wilson – talked to our reporter – said experts had examined part of the building – council had said the walls were unsafe – experts said the walls only needed a few simple repairs – any local builder could do them! – money (given by supporters of the campaign) almost enough for repairs – many people heard about the campaign – publicised by local radio stations: criticised the Council (Council's decision not widely publicised!) – Robin Wilson now looking for volunteers: come and help do the necessary repair work (it will take about four weeks) – chairman (*Vorsitzende/r*) of Council committee (he made the decision): very angry – Robin Wilson (local people admire him) – got married last week – met his wife (comes from London) as a result of his campaign work – both dynamic people – Council chairman dislikes them!

9.4 *Which* als satzbezügliches Pronomen

Which kennst du schon als Relativpronomen bei Dingen/Sachen.

› The book **which** I'm reading is by John Wain.	(*notwendiger Relativsatz*)
This book, **which** cost me £10, is very interesting.	(*nicht-notwendiger Relativsatz*)

Eine weitere Funktion von *which* ist die Zusammenfassung eines vorangehenden Hauptsatzes im Sinne des deutschen „was".

› Sie trug einen Rock, **den** ich sehr schön fand.	(Hier finde ich nur den Rock schön.)
Sie trug einen Rock, **was** ich sehr schön fand.	(Hier finde ich die Aussage des ganzen Hauptsatzes – die Tatsache, dass sie einen Rock trug – schön.)
Der Zahnarzt zog zwei Zähne, **die** mir wehtaten.	(Die Zähne taten mir vorher weh.)
Der Zahnarzt zog zwei Zähne, **was** mir wehtat.	(Das Ziehen der Zähne tat mir weh.)
She was wearing a skirt **which** I thought was very nice.	(notwendiger Relativsatz; Das Relativpronomen *which* bezieht sich nur auf den Rock.)
She was wearing a skirt, **which** I thought was very nice.	(*which* in satzbezüglicher Funktion; Also bezieht sich *which* hier auf die Aussage den ganzen Hauptsatzes.)

Relativsätze, die mit dem satzbezüglichen *which* eingeleitet werden, sind immer **nicht-notwendig**, da sie nur einen Kommentar zum Hauptsatz abgeben.

Aufgabe 7

Use *which* to join the sentence pairs. Don't forget the comma!

1. I told him I had no money. This was perfectly true.
   I told him I had no money, which was perfectly true.
2. She said she couldn't help me. It was just an excuse.
3. He arrived half an hour late. That was very impolite of him.
4. My sister watches TV a lot. Watching so much TV is not good for her.
5. Last week I went to a family wedding. I usually hate family weddings!
6. All my cousins were there. This made the wedding more fun.
7. Even my great-grandmother was there. This fact astonished everyone.
8. The old lady is 99 years old. Her amazing age makes her the oldest member of our family.
9. When my father saw my last school report, he got very angry. That didn't surprise me.
10. I had bad marks in most subjects. I couldn't explain this fact.
11. Luckily I had a 2 in English. This amazing result surprised my father.
12. He told me his best mark for English at school had been a 3. This shocked me.
13. His marks in other subjects had been bad too! I didn't know this!

Aufgabe 8

How is *which* used in the following sentences: sentence related or a relative pronoun in a relative clause? Put the commas in the right places.

1. This is the book which I was telling you about. I read it in three days which is very fast for me! It's a story about a pop group which started at our school.
2. Tom suggested a party which I thought was a good idea. Then Jenny suggested a barbecue which sounded like an even better idea. She said she had plenty of food left from the barbecue which they had had at the weekend.
3. He said he played the guitar in a pop group which was very good. His sister said that she was a singer in the same group which is nonsense. My friend John told me it was a true story which I didn't believe. But he has often told me stories which I didn't believe.

9.5 *What* als Relativpronomen

Im Gegensatz zum satzbezüglichen *which* als Entsprechung zum deutschen „was" wird die deutsche Konstruktion „(das,) was …" im Englischen mit *what* wiedergegeben.

› **(Das,) was** er mir sagte, ist wahr.	**What** he told me is true.
Was du nicht weißt, ist, dass er oft lügt.	**What** you don't know is that he often tells lies.
Aber ich glaube immer **das**, **was** er mir erzählt.	But I always believe **what** he tells me.

Das englische Wort *what* wird also nicht nur in Fragen benutzt, sondern auch, um ein Nomen zu ersetzen oder zu erweitern. In diesen Sätzen könnte der erste Teil des Satzes durch ein Nomen ersetzt werden.

› **What he told me** is true.
= **His story** is true.

What you don't know is that he often tells lies.
= **The truth** is that he often tells lies.

But I always believe **what he tells me**.
= But I always believe **his stories**.

Besonders am Satzanfang und gelegentlich in der Satzmitte wird im Deutschen das einführende „das" oft weggelassen. Im Englischen brauchst du in solchen Sätzen immer nur das Pronomen *what*.

Aufgabe 9

Use the *what*-construction to replace the bold parts of the sentences. Use a suitable verb instead of the bold words. Use the right tense and don't forget *what* is used in the singular.

1. I found it hard to understand **his wishes**.
   I found it hard to understand what he wanted.

2. I find it hard to believe **his stories**.

   ____

3. **The thing that** is important is to learn ten new words a day.

   ____

4. Tell me something about **your mum's job**.

   ____

5. **His actions** were hard to explain.

   ____

6. I watched him carefully but couldn't observe **his actions** exactly.

   ____

7. **Their suggestions** were out of the question.

   ____

8. Three strong men are **necessary** to move this piano.

   ____

9. A big portion of fish and chips is precisely **my wish**.

   ____

10. **Your thoughts** are not important. **Your actions** are.

    ____

11. **The things that** go on at my school would surprise you!

    ____

Abschlusstest online 9

Perfekt! Du hast **Kapitel 9 – Relativsätze** durchgearbeitet. Du kennst den Unterschied zwischen bestimmenden und nicht bestimmenden Relativsätzen und kennst dich mit Relativpronomen gut aus, egal ob sie als Subjekt oder als Objekt vorkommen.

So funktioniert der Abschlusstest online:
Um deinen Lernerfolg zu überprüfen, kannst du nun die Tests online machen. Gehe auf
www.klasse5bis10.klett-lerntraining.de/5X7F
und registriere dich wie vorne im Buch beschrieben.

Welche Tests es gibt, siehst du unten in der Tabelle. Nach jedem Test bekommst du eine Auswertung.

Willst du immer im Blick haben, welche Themen du schon kannst oder was du besser nochmal wiederholen solltest? Dann notiere deine Ergebnisse aus den Abschlusstests in der Tabelle.

Mein Ergebnis im Abschlusstest – Kapitel 9

Thema	Mein Ergebnis
Relativsätze	

Lösungen

1 Adjektiv und Adverb

Aufgabe 1

a) Adverbs
   1. with verbs:
      will be lowered **gently** – flies **faster** than – can move as **fast** as – leap **vertically** – are **gradually** being explored – **easily** contain – will **far** outweigh – will benefit **immediately**
   2. with adjectives:
      equally great – **Majestically** moving
   3. with other adverbs:
      much more … than – **fairly** regularly

b) Adjectives
   the **last** frontier – a **revolutionary new** submarine – **first** voyage – **Deep** Flight I – **other deep-sea** research vessels – the … **highest** mountain – **manned** voyages … have become **common** – the **deepest** parts – are **most interested** in – the **deepest** parts – **little** is known about the **middle** waters – the … **last great** frontier – **more** life by weight – **other** ecosystem – their **economic** potential is equally **great** – **moving** ocean currents – **weather-related** disasters – **many valuable** minerals and **other** substances – discoveries **helpful** to

Aufgabe 2

1. carefully 2. brave 3. well 4. complicated; only 5. very slowly 6. safely 7. soon 8. dramatically 9. old 10. remotely; quickly 11. expensive 12. scientific 13. marine 14. completely 15. imperfect 16. endless 17. closely 18. astonishingly deep

Aufgabe 3

Across: 5. useful 6. quickly 8. unhappy 9. far 10. carefully
Down: 1. quick 2. well 3. slowly 4. loud 7. sure 9. full 11. awful 12. early

Aufgabe 4

1. **good** snack bar; really **well**; **better** than; the **best** place
2. be **worse** than; the **worst** salads; doing **badly**
3. **more interesting** than
4. was **happy**; is **happier**; the **happiest** people; very **happy**
5. find it **more difficult** than; it's **less difficult** than; the **most difficult** language
6. have **much** time; had **more** time; as **much** money; **many** hobbies; **more** carefully
7. have **less** time; has a **little** time; watches **less** than; watches the **least** TV
8. feel **good** today; feel **better** than; would be **best/better**; work **best/better**; do **better**; did so **badly**; my **worst** exams; you'd **better**; won't do **well**; will be **worse** than
9. **extreme** views; **extremely** strict; more **extreme** than; the **most extreme** headmaster

Aufgabe 5

1. *Adverb bzw. adverbiale Bestimmung am Satzanfang:*
   Sometimes there is high grass in a field – **Always** ask permission before you camp

2. *Adverb bzw. adverbiale Bestimmung am Satz- oder Satzteilende:*
   it will be difficult for the farmer to cut the hay **later** – It is probably best to ask the farmer **first** – Dozens of sheep and lambs are killed **on British farms each year**

3. *Adverb vor dem Vollverb (ohne Adverbien der Art und Weise):*
   you should **always** observe The Country Code – You should **never** walk across fields – Most paths are **clearly** marked. – Farmers don't **usually** mind – If you **thoughtlessly** walk across this field – Farmers will not **often** refuse permission – even though they **almost always** charge a small sum – Dogs **often** run after other animals – A strange dog will **certainly** frighten farm animals and may **possibly** injure them

4. *Adverbien der Art und Weise:*
   Most paths are **clearly** marked. – If you **thoughtlessly** walk across this field – Follow them **carefully** – which a farmer has planted **specially** – their owners have not kept them **properly under control**

Folgendes Adverb passt nicht in eine der obigen Kategorien: unless you are **perfectly** sure (Adverb bestimmt Adjektiv)

Aufgabe 6

1. We often go to bed at ten o'clock. / At ten o'clock we often …
2. They have always lived in London.
3. Next year we are flying to Spain in the autumn.
4. Luckily he was not driving his car very fast.
5. She has never been to London in December.
6. I rarely watch TV at the weekends.
7. Yesterday he nearly drove his new e-scooter into a wall. / He … yesterday.
8. Do you often come to the youth club on Fridays?

Aufgabe 7

1. When we arrived at the campsite it was terribly late.
2. But we had often stayed at this site before, so that was no problem.
3. We put up our tent unbelievably quickly and were in our sleeping bags soon afterwards.
4. About an hour later I woke up. / I woke up about an hour later.
5. I could hear someone walking quietly around the campsite.
6. My friend Tom was snoring loudly beside me.
7. He is a heavy sleeper.
8. Perhaps the warden was quickly making a last check / … was making a last quick check before going happily to his own bed.
9. Then I heard very quiet voices.
10. A man and a woman were talking softly to each other.
11. "This is an absolutely impossible place!" said the man.
12. "We can't possibly put up our tent here in the middle of the night. People are trying to sleep!"
13. "If we had left early and arrived here before midnight everything would have been OK."
14. "Now we'll have to get up early and ask the warden if we can stay. It's all your fault."
15. "Why is it always my fault?" asked the man. "You're the one who is so terribly keen on camping!"
16. "Be quiet!" whispered the woman. "You'll wake someone up."
17. They didn't know that they had already woken me up. / … woken me up already.

Aufgabe 8

Lösungsvorschlag:

1. The weather was very **bright** when we arrived in the Scottish Highlands. The sun was shining **brightly**.
2. We were very **happy**. We cycled **happily** along/through the countryside.
3. We cycled **carefully** down a steep hill. / We were very **careful** because the hill was very steep.
4. It was still very **early** when we arrived at Loch Ness. / When we arrived at Loch Ness it was still very **early**.
5. We felt very **lazy**, so we lay **lazily** on the bank of the lake/Loch Ness in the sunshine.
6. **Suddenly** Nessie, the Loch Ness Monster, appeared. / We **suddenly** saw Nessie, the Loch Ness Monster.

7. **Quickly** I / I **quickly** picked up my camera.
8. Nessie was swimming **calmly** on the surface of the loch/lake.
9. We were very **excited**. We got on our bikes and cycled **excitedly** to the office of the Inverness News.
10. **Unluckily** we dropped the camera. / **Unluckily** the camera fell on the floor. We were very **unlucky**. (= Wir hatten großes Pech.)
    We didn't have much luck! We had been very **unlucky**! (= Wir hatten großes Pech gehabt.)
    We were very **unhappy** (nicht: unlucky) about our bad **luck**!

Aufgabe 9

1. The CD sounded loud/terrible.
2. We looked carefully at the picture. / … at the picture carefully.
3. She screamed terribly at the picture / when she saw my homework.
4. The explorers felt their way carefully along the tunnel.
5. Jackie gave a loud/terrible scream.
6. My teacher criticized me angrily / screamed terribly when she/he saw my homework.
7. The food smelt/tasted delicious/terrible/unusual.
8. The visitors looked carefully at the picture.
9. Her singing sounded beautiful/terrible.
10. I felt terrible after my flight. / I gave a terrible scream.

Aufgabe 10

1. high-flying aircraft
2. well-dressed person
3. long-lasting battery
4. well-organized rock concert
5. badly-prepared lesson
6. sweet-smelling rose
7. attractive-looking person
8. fast-moving vehicle
9. badly-scratched display
10. low-lying ground

2 Zeitformen zur Wiedergabe von Gegenwart und Zukunft

Aufgabe 1

1 a), 2 c), 3 b), 4 a), 5 b), 6 a)

Aufgabe 2

1. My mother is not working in an office at present / at the moment. (Ort vor Zeit!)
2. Jan and Marie play tennis every week.
3. Do you always go to school at half past seven?
4. He's always playing his violin!
5. They are learning Spanish now / at the moment.
6. Does she never go swimming?
7. He rarely listens to jazz.
8. Next week I'm going to a rock concert.
9. The last bus leaves at midnight.

Aufgabe 3

Simple form:

The Channel coast … **has** some of the finest beaches (*kein Hilfsverb hier!*) – The White Cliffs of Dover **stand** guard – people who **want** to explore the countryside – Devon and Cornwall **lie** in the extreme south-west of England. – Visit Dartmoor and Exmoor, where ponies still **live** wild. – Cornwall **possesses** many interesting relics – (Cornwall) **is** still the home of china clay mining. (*kein Hilfsverb hier!*) – This **is** the Heart of England. (*kein Hilfsverb!*) – Every year many thousands of people **visit** the home of … – Tourists **love** the lovely stone houses – which they **find** in the Cotswolds. – places which **have** names like … – But the charm of the Cotswolds **does** not **end** with … – Visitors **come** from all over Europe … – Who **says** there is nothing to see … – … from the centre of Manchester **lies** some of England's prettiest moorland scenery. – It **runs** from Carlisle on the west coast to Newcastle … and **is** the biggest single national monument in Britain.

Progressive form:

If you **are planning** a holiday with a difference – … that **are waiting** to welcome you. – **Are** you **thinking** of spending longer than a week here? – Yorkshire … and its capital, York … **are waiting** to be discovered. – What **are** you **waiting** for? – We **are looking** forward to seeing you in England next year!

Modal auxiliaries:

You **can** explore the quiet country lanes in your own car. – Then you **might** like to rent one of the holiday flats – which **are to** be found in most of the larger towns. – Who **could** resist places which have names like …

Aufgabe 4

1. aren't listening 2. go; we are going 3. 're/are having 4. They have 5. are they staying 6. have 7. take 8. are driving 9. are they coming 10. Do you know 11. don't think 12. does she live 13. 's/is staying 14. Do you mean; always arrives 15. believe; 's/is 16. don't see 17. are you 18. owes; need

Aufgabe 5

Lösungsvorschlag:

Dear Rob, / Dear Anna,

My name is … and I live in …

1. At the moment I am writing to you!
2. I am fifteen years old / a fan of techno music.
3. Sometimes my family (and I) go out for a meal / go for a walk in the countryside.
4. Every week we/I visit our/my friends in …
5. We are usually at home on Sundays.
6. On Saturdays we never go to school / always go shopping.
7. I never forget to do my homework.
8. During the week we usually have lunch at home.

Aufgabe 6

2. a) "**Are** you **going (to go)** to London next week?"
   b) "(Please) **Will** you **buy** me a souvenir?
3. a) "**Shall** I **open** the window?"
   b) "**Will** the traffic noise **be** too loud?"
4. a) "**Aren't** you **going to offer** me one?"
   b) "You**'ll have** a stomach ache if you eat them all!"
5. a) "OK, I**'ll go**!"
   b) "**Aren't** you **going to answer** the door?"

Aufgabe 7

2. "I'**m** not **going to stop**."
3. "Nobody **will see** me if I walk away."
4. "Someone **will arrive** in a few minutes. I**'ll be** late for school if I wait any longer!"
5. "**Shall** I **call** an ambulance?"
6. "Don't move! I**'m going to call** an ambulance!"
7. "OK, I **wont move**."
8. "I hope she **will be** OK."
9. "**Shall** we try and get her out?"
10. "I'**m** not **going to move** her."
11. "**Will** you **call** the police too?"
12. "Yes, OK, it **won't take** long!"

Aufgabe 8

1. Sue will be travelling to Birmingham.
2. John will be ironing his shirts.
3. Mrs Baker will be reading the paper.
4. Mr Baker will be sitting in the garden.
5. Julia will be washing her hair.
6. The girls will be playing football.
7. Our teacher will be teaching (us) English.
8. Chloe and Anna will be listening to the music.
9. Our cat will be having (its) lunch.

Aufgabe 9

1. + h) What will you do if you can't find the key?
2. + e) What will you be doing this time next week?
3. + g) Don't hit him or he'll tell the police!
4. + b) Don't disturb him because he'll probably be sleeping.
5. + j) Will they be having lunch when we arrive?
6. + f) Will they have lunch before we arrive?
7. + i) If we arrive late they will be having breakfast.
8. + c) When we arrive we will all have breakfast.
9. + a) She'll finish work at exactly ten past five.
10. + d) She'll be finishing work about now.

Andere Kombinationen sind auch möglich, z.B.:
1. + f) What will you do before we arrive?
2. + j) What will you be doing when we arrive?

Die alternativen Sätze bei 5 und 6 klingen allerdings dann etwas seltsam:
5. + e) Will they be having lunch this time next week?
6. + h) Will they have lunch if you can't find the key?

Aufgabe 10

1. I will have passed my driving test.
2. she will have finished her training.
3. we will have been living / will have lived there for 10 years.
4. will you have been learning English
5. 'll/will have been talking
6. won't have been waiting
7. will have marked
8. 'll/will have been saving
9. 'll/will have saved enough
10. Will they have arrived
11. will have been working
12. will have finished working
13. 'll/will have finished building
14. 'll/will have been studying English
15. 'll/will have drunk

3 Zeitformen der Vergangenheit

Aufgabe 1

A light rain **was falling** when I **reached** the station. – It was while I **was looking** for a seat that I **saw** her. – … and as I **was watching** I suddenly **saw** a young man … – But the train **was travelling** quite fast now, so he **couldn't catch** it. – Before five minutes **had passed**, Alicia and I **were talking** as if … – By the time we **were passing** through York, I **knew** that I had found myself a new girlfriend. – I **looked** up … and **saw** that Rosie **was walking** quickly …

Aufgabe 2

Background description:
I **was going** home after my first term at university, and I **was feeling** very happy.
I **was studying** in Edinburgh and my parents were **living** in London.
I **was** very much **looking** forward to going home
Many of my friends **were travelling** south on the same train,
The girl of my dreams **was sitting** there **reading** a paperback novel,
The train **was** still **standing** at the platform.
Other young people **were putting** their bags … between the seats
He **was running** after the train.
She **was facing** the other way.
She **was** not **smiling**.

was …-ing = wollte
I **was keeping** this seat free for my boyfriend,
she **was staying** with an uncle and aunt over Christmas

One other progressive form is used. Did you write it down?
It is not a past progressive form, so don't worry if you didn't find it:
because my girlfriend Rosie **would be meeting** me at Kings Cross Station.

Aufgabe 3

1. + g) She was talking to me when the phone rang.
2. + j) Before the robber entered the bank, she put a mask on.
3. + i) When we went on holiday, we always locked all the doors.
4. + a) John talked to Sheila when they met at the pub.
5. + h) First they bought the tickets, then they got on the train.
6. + d) While we were playing tennis, all our clothes were stolen.
7. + b) The boys grilled the meat while the girls were watching TV.
8. + c) When I last saw the bank robber, she was wearing a mask.
9. + e) They were on the platform when the train arrived.
10. + f) The boys were grilling the meat when the dog stole the sausages.

Aufgabe 4

1. waited 2. were waiting 3. did you say 4. was talking 5. was saying 6. saw
7. was doing 8. was seeing 9. talked 10. did she do 11. had 12. was having

Aufgabe 5

1. While I was walking to school one morning, I saw an accident.
2. Just as I was crossing the road, a car drove into / hit another car.
3. When the police arrived, the two drivers were arguing / shouting at each other.
4. While the two police officers were just getting out of their car, one of the drivers hit the other driver.
5. While the driver who had been hit was lying on the ground, the other driver ran off.
6. Just as he was running round the corner, he ran into / hit a big man.
7. While the driver was getting up, one of the police officers caught him.

Aufgabe 6

1. Simple past – completed period of time is given or is clear from the context
Violent confrontations between police and Asian youths **provoked** widespread shock last weekend. The campaign **began** in Birmingham last year. When repeated complaints … **produced** no results, Asians **set up** vigilante groups to clean up the areas. The violent confrontation with police in Bradford last weekend **showed** that …

2. Present perfect – action still going on
Over the past few years Asians in Britain … **have felt** very worried … … there **have been** many cases of crimes … A sex magazine with photos of Asian girls **has been** in circulation for over a year, … *Young Asians **have taken over** the … campaign … and **made** it more militant.

3. Present perfect – action (or actions) completed at an undefined time in the past
… the way in which the wider culture … **has invaded** the areas where they live. Drug-taking **has increased** within the Asian community, … All this … **has generated** a climate of moral panic. *Many Asians living in city centres **have found** that the value of their houses goes down … Muslims **have started** a campaign to protect themselves … *This **has led** to a conflict of values and ways of life. Many of them **have left** school without adequate qualifications, … … they **have adopted** Western values …

4. Present perfect – action takes place in the present or very close to the present
a gay magazine for Asians **has** just **appeared**

*Die mit * gekennzeichneten Sätze in den Abschnitten 2 und 3 könnten auch im jeweils anderen Abschnitt eingeordnet werden.*

Aufgabe 7

Lösungsvorschläge:

play:
We played "hide and seek" as children. – I played "hide and seek" as a child. – Did you ever play "hide and seek" as a child? – Have you ever played football? – I/We often play football.

visit:
Did you visit London last year? – We/I visited London last year. – Have you visited Frankfurt yet? – I/We have never visited Frankfurt. – We/I haven't visited Frankfurt yet.

eat:
Have you ever eaten fish and chips? – We/I have often eaten fish and chips. – Did you eat marmalade when you were in England? – I/We often ate marmalade when we were in England.

listen to:
Did you listen to the radio yesterday evening? – I/We listened to the radio yesterday evening. – We've / I've often listened to concerts on the radio. – I/We have never listened to concerts on the radio. – Have you ever listened to concerts on the radio?

drink:
Did you ever drink beer when you were younger? – We/I never drank beer when we were / I was younger.

watch:
Did you watch a horror film last night? – I watched a horror film last night.

Aufgabe 8

1. has gone; went
2. have lived; lived
3. Did you do; Have you done
4. did not drive; have not driven
5. learnt; have not learnt
6. wrote; has written
7. have bought; bought
8. Have you often drunk; Did you often drink
9. Has Julie ever flown; did she fly
10. Have you seen; Did you see

Aufgabe 9

1. We have seen this film twice.
2. We saw this film last week.
3. He lived / was living in Berlin when I knew him.
4. My aunt works / is working in an office.
5. My uncle has worked / has been working in Spain since 2015.
6. Our teacher has visited / been to England three times.
7. He has lived / has been living here for four years.
8. He lived here for a year before he went / before going to the USA.
9. She has just arrived.
10. She always arrives punctually / on time.

Aufgabe 10

… the White Tower, **was** built by William the Conqueror … **has been** used as a palace, a prison … Many people **have been** imprisoned or executed … including Anne Boleyn … who **was** beheaded here … Her ghost and many others **have been** seen

Aufgabe 11

1. has always had
2. was; was
3. worked; did not live; preferred
4. was built
5. was called; have taken over
6. ran; was

Aufgabe 12

Jenny: Yes. I packed it yesterday. – Have you bought the food?

Paul: Yes / Of course. I bought it this afternoon. – (But) Have you packed your rucksack?

Jenny: I haven't finished (packing it) yet. I'm just doing / packing it.
or: Yes. I've just packed / finished packing it.
– Have you phoned the camp site (yet)?

Paul: Yes. I phoned it yesterday.

Aufgabe 13

2. I've been playing football.
3. she has been living in London for three years already.
4. have you been waiting here?
5. someone has been drinking it!
6. 've/have been practising English grammar since three o'clock.
7. has she been doing all afternoon?
8. I've been looking forward to it all week!
9. Has the baby been behaving well?

Aufgabe 14

1. Have you learnt
2. have you been learning
3. I haven't seen
4. has been seeing
5. have been having
6. have never had
7. has been working
8. have worked
9. have you been doing … 've / have been listening
10. have you done 11. Have you been playing
12. Have you ever been

Aufgabe 15

Present perfect sentences:

1. John has been learning English / living here John has lived / has been working here	since last June.
2. We have been learning English / living here We have lived / have been working here	for three years/months.
3. She has been learning English / living here She has lived / has been working here	for six weeks.
4. They have been learning English / living here They have been working here	since they left Berlin.
5. Peter and Sophia have been learning English / living here Peter and Sophia have lived / have been working here	since three months/years ago.

Simple past sentences:

5. John / We / She / They / Peter and Sophia came / lived here	three months/ years ago/for six weeks.

Other answers are also possible, but not simple past tense + "since"

Aufgabe 16

1. For 2. ago 3. since; since 4. from 5. Since 6. For 7. from 8. ago 9. since 10. since

Aufgabe 17

1. … even though this service **has been running for** fifty years.
2. They say **that there has always been a bus service and that they have always used the buses**. One woman says **she has been using the bus since 1958**.
3. She is talking to some of the villagers. **"Have you written to the bus company?"** – "Yes, **but we haven't had / received a reply yet**."
4. "Well, **we have decided to take over the bus service (ourselves)**.
5. I **have worked / been working on the buses since 1994**." – "Yes. I think I'm a good driver because **I've had a/my driving licence for 9 years**.
6. and **I've never had an accident / I've not had an accident yet**."
7. The villagers of Strathdon **have been discussing the problem for two and a half hours**.
8. A representative of the bus company **has just arrived**.
9. We **have had a frank and open exchange of views** but no real progress **has been made**.
10. The bus company **has decided to let them try for (a period of) three weeks**."

Aufgabe 18

2. **Have** you **seen** my school bag (anywhere)? 3. **Have** you **been eating** my chocolate?
4. Who **has eaten** (all) my chocolate? 5. **Have** you **seen** Dave Smith recently?
6. **Have** you **been waiting** (for me) long? 7. How long **has** he **been living** here?
8. Where **have** you **been**? 9. What **have** you **done**? 10. What **have** you **been doing**?
11. How long **have** you **been practising** English?

Aufgabe 19

2. **After** Ella **had passed** her driving test, she bought a car.
3. **After** she **had driven** home, she locked the car and went into the house.
4. **After** Ella **had made** a cup of coffee, she phoned her friend Anna.
5. She put down the phone **after** she **had said** goodbye to Anna.
6. She looked out of the window **after** she **had heard** a loud noise.
7. Two young men were trying to steal her car **after** they **had broken** a window to get into the car.
8. **After** Ella **had realised** what was happening, she rang the police.
9. Her neighbour came out of his house **after** he **had heard** the noise.
10. **After** the man **had shouted** something, the boys looked up and saw him.
11. **After** they **had run** away, a police car arrived outside Ella's house.

Aufgabe 20

1. **When** he told me his name, I knew who he was.
2. **When** we **had** finished lunch, we went for a walk.
3. **When** she **had** wiped her feet on the doormat, she shut the front door.
4. **When** he took the dog for a walk, it was very cold outside.
5. **When** we **had** finished the test, our teacher collected our exercise books.
6. My mum learnt Russian **when** she went to school in East Germany.
7. **When** the sun **had** set, the stars came out.
8. I lit a candle **when** the lights went out.
9. **When** he tried to speak French, everybody laughed.
10. **When** all my friends were on holiday, I felt very lonely.

Aufgabe 21

1. After we **had flown** from London to New York, we booked into a hotel in Manhattan.
2. After we **had been** on / **had taken** a sightseeing trip round Manhattan, we went to see the Statue of Liberty.
3. After we **had celebrated** Independence Day in New York City, we went by car / drove to Washington.
4. After/When we **had seen** the sights of Washington, we went/flew/drove to Disneyworld in Orlando, Florida.
5. After/When we **had spent** two days in Florida, we flew to Arizona.
6. After/When we **had visited** the Grand Canyon, we went to / visited Yosemite National Park.
7. After/When we **had driven** over the Rockies to San Francisco, we stayed with friends there.
8. After/When we **had seen** the Golden Gate Bridge and the other sights, we flew on to Seattle.
9. After/When we **had spent** two days in Seattle with friends of Alan's, we flew back to London via Chicago.
10. After/When we **had recovered** from the jet lag, we felt much better!

Aufgabe 22

1. **Before** he **had finished** his lunch, his guests arrived.
   or: He (had) finished his lunch **before** his guests arrived.
2. She bought a newspaper **before** the train left.
3. We put warm clothes on **before** we went out into the snow.
4. The boy jumped off **before** the bus **had stopped**.
5. The TV programme started **before** we **had finished** our homework.
   or: **Before** the TV programme started, we finished our homework.
6. We (had) reached home **before** it began to rain.
7. **Before** they **had reached** the bus station, the bus left.
8. She left school **before** she **had finished** her course.
9. They left New York **before** they **had had** time to see the Statue of Liberty.
10. **Before** we **had started** to eat, the others arrived.

Aufgabe 23

Johnny Brown, a famous pop singer, was born in 1984. After he **had left** school in 2000, he started work as an assistant in a music shop. When he **had been learning** to play the guitar for three years, he joined the Max Miller Band, which he left after he **had** only **been playing** with for two months. After he **had been living** in New York for three years, he founded The Kriggs. When the group **had been playing** together for two years, it broke up. After he **had solved** his drug problem, he founded a new group The Days. Their first concert was so successful that they could only leave the stage after they **had given** six encores. They made their first CD in 2012 after their fans **had been waiting** / (**had waited**) for two years! The group **had been working** together for three years when they broke up in 2014. They **had given** twenty concerts and made three CDs.

4 Bedingungssätze

Aufgabe 1

1. I **will** visit New York.
2. if you **invite** us.
3. we**'ll have**
4. we **pick** them **up** at the station / **fetch** them from the station.
5. if I **give** it you
6. you **will (not)** / **won't enjoy**
7. **Will** you **help** me … if I **help you in the garden**
8. **if I've saved**
9. **run** faster, the others **will catch** us!

Aufgabe 2

1. may/might/can 2. could 3. could 4. should 5. may/might 6. must/have to 7. might 8. needn't 9. can 10. mustn't/shouldn't

Aufgabe 3

1. + e) 2. + d) 3. + a) 4. + f) 5. + b) 6.+c) 7. + i) 8. + g) 9. + j) 10. + h)

Aufgabe 4

1. will probably visit 2. would see 3. were 4. Would … go 5. would see 6. wasn't/was not 7. wouldn't/would not be 8. wouldn't/would not pollute 9. wouldn't/would not happen 10. Would … visit

Aufgabe 5

Type I:

I**'ll go** to university and study Business Studies if I **get** the right marks.

If you **want to** find a volunteer project, you **will find** so much information on the internet.

… if you **know** roughly what you want to do, it **will make** things easier.

If I **don't feel** better soon, I**'ll have to** change my flight and go home.

If you **do** a volunteer project, you**'ll never forget** it.

Type II:

If you thought I **was** just **talking** about booking your flight and packing your suitcase, you **would be** very wrong.

You **would be** advised to get a weekend or part-time job if you **haven't got** one.

If I **got** the chance, I **would volunteer** for the same project again.

Type III:

If you **had asked** me a year ago, what I **would have done** after school …

I **would have asked** my grandparents for a loan, if I **hadn't saved** enough money, …

If I **had had** problems, I **would have known** who to go to.

Aufgabe 6

2. If he had bought new tyres, he wouldn't have had a puncture.
3. If he hadn't had a puncture, he wouldn't have got wet.
4. If he hadn't got wet, he wouldn't have caught a cold.
5. If he hadn't caught a cold, he wouldn't have moved into the B & B.
6. If he hadn't moved into the B & B, he wouldn't have met Claire.
7. If he hadn't met Claire, he wouldn't have climbed the hill.
8. If he hadn't climbed the hill, he wouldn't have hurt his ankle.
9. If he hadn't hurt his ankle, his holiday wouldn't have been spoilt.

Aufgabe 7

2. If I **had won** a prize, I **wouldn't be** unhappy.
3. John **wouldn't be living** in London now if he **hadn't found** a job there last year.
4. If my friend **hadn't started** learning French a couple of years ago, he **wouldn't spend** his holidays there regularly.
5. If you **liked** the group's last CD, you**'ll love** this one!
6. You **won't know** Alice if you **weren't** at my party last year.
7. If he **hadn't emigrated** to Australia when he was a boy, he **wouldn't be** a wealthy farmer now.
8. If she **hadn't learned** to speak Arabic when she was a girl, she **wouldn't be working** in Beirut now.
9. If you **bought** your mountain bike three years ago, you **will need** a new one now!
10. How **will** you **recognise** him if you**'ve** never **seen** him before?
11. "If they **have** never **been** there, they **won't know** the place."

Aufgabe 8

1. We can have a break when this exercise is done.
2. She'll pass her exams if they aren't too hard.
3. I might go to Venezuela if my parents pay for my ticket.
4. You should talk to Jean if you want to learn French.
5. They could go to Spain if the flights are cheap.
6. We can get married when we are 18.
7. She'd get a better job if she could speak Spanish.
8. I have no idea when he'll be arriving.
9. You'll remember him when you see him again.

5 Die indirekte Rede

Aufgabe 1

2. The teacher / My mum / … asked us / me / … to stop talking.
3. The teacher / shop assistant / police officer / … ordered / told him/her/me/us/… to empty his/her/my/our/… pockets.
4. The captain ordered / commanded the crew / passengers to abandon (the) ship.
5. The police officer/detective told/ordered the taxi driver/motorist to follow that/the robbers' car.
6. The salesperson advised/recommended the customer to wash this/that/the T-shirt in warm water only. or: … only to wash … water.
7. My/His/Her/mum/dad told me/him/her not to hit my/his/her sister.
8. The driving instructor/teacher told/warned/advised his/her student to always look over his/her shoulder when reversing.
9. The PE teacher warned/told the students never to come into the gym …
10. Our maths teacher / … ordered / shouted at / told us to be quiet and sit down.
11. I/He/She/… asked him/her/me/… to meet me/him/her/… at the station.
12. The advertisement/poster recommended people/readers/passersby to buy … .
13. He/She/I/… begged me/her/him/… not to drive so fast.
14. The police officer/robber told/ordered the people/us/me/… to put up their/ our/my/… hands and (to) stand perfectly still.
15. The fire officers/people shouted about the fire.
16. Our teacher/… begged us to pay attention.

Aufgabe 2

1. Yesterday Kate's mother **asked her to go** to the shop and buy her a kilo of rice and a few other things.
2. Her little brother Tommy **begged her to take him to the shop with her**.
3. Kate agreed but **warned/told him not to ask for any sweets**.
4. In the shop Kate **told/warned Tommy not to touch anything**.
5. Then Tommy **wanted/asked Kate to buy him** an ice lolly, but Kate said no.
6. Tommy started to cry, but Kate **begged him not to cry in the shop**.
7. After that, Kate **told Tommy/her brother to wait for her at the cash desk**.
8. The shopkeeper **warned an old lady / shouted to an old lady to look out**.
9. Then the shopkeeper **asked/requested Kate to leave his shop**.
10. Outside, Kate **ordered/told Tommy never to do that again**.

Aufgabe 3

a) 2. He/She says he/she **lives** in a flat.
3. He/She says he/she **likes** techno music.
4. He/She says he/she **has** got two brothers and a sister.
5. He/She says his/her hobbies **are** football and skateboarding.
6. He/She says he/she **plays** in a club.
7. He/She says he/she **doesn't** go to school on Saturdays any more.
8. He/She says he/she **hasn't been** to America yet.
9. He/She says he/she only **started** English a year ago.
10. He/She says he/she **likes** it over here.
11. He/She says he/she **is** going back to Germany in two weeks.
12. He/She says he/she **was** playing football.
13. He/She says she/the girl **is** Mia and that she **comes** from Dortmund too. He/She says she/Mia **came** to the park after she **had done** her homework.

b) 1. He/She said he/she lived near Dortmund.
2. He/She said he/she **lived** in a flat.
3. He/She said he/she **liked** techno music.
4. He/She said he/she **had** got two brothers and a sister.
5. He/She said his/her hobbies **were** football and skateboarding.
6. He/She said he/she **played** in a club.
7. He/She said he/she **didn't** go to school on Saturdays any more.
8. He/She said he/she **hadn't been** to America yet.
9. He/She said he/she had only **started** English a year ago.
10. He/She said he/she **liked** it over here.
11. He/She said he/she **was** going back to Germany in two weeks.
12. He/She said he/she **had been** playing football.
13. He/She said she/the girl **was** Mia and that she **came** from Dortmund too. He/She said she/Mia **had come** to the park after she had **done** her homework.

Aufgabe 4

3. a) She said (that) she **was** staying **here tonight**.
b) She told me yesterday morning she **was** staying **here for the night / on Sunday night**.
c) On Sunday she informed me that she **was** staying **there / in Leeds for the night / on Sunday night**.

4. a) Peter told me that he **had seen** John **here on Monday / the day before yesterday**.
b) Peter told me that he **had seen** John **in London on Monday**.
c) Peter rang me and said that he **had seen** John **here yesterday**.

Aufgabe 5

2. Our teacher told us (that) he **had** to go and see the headteacher, **so** he asked us **to take** out our books and do the exercise on page 23. *or:* Our teacher asked us **to take** out our books … **because** he **had** to go and see the headteacher.
3. My mother asked me **to give** her my dirty jeans **because** she **wanted** to wash them.
4. My brother told me/said he **had lent** me £2 and asked me **to give** it him back.
5. My sister told me **to take** that/the T-shirt off because it **was** hers.
6. My friend asked me **to have** another biscuit and told me / **because** he / she **had** got plenty.
7. The/A police officer told/warned us that the/this road **had been flooded** and asked us **to follow** the DIVERSION signs.
8. My uncle asked me **to come** in and **sit** down. Then he asked me **to have** a cup of tea and said/told me that/**because** he **hadn't been** expecting me so early.
9. The ticket inspector told me that the/this ticket **was** only valid with a Young Person's Railcard, **so** he asked me to show him my Railcard.
10. My/Her ex-boyfriend told me/her **to go** home **because** he **hadn't invited** me/her to his party.
11. The notice advised us **to avoid** the last-minute rush and **to post** early for Christmas. *or*: … to avoid the last-minute rush **by posting** early for Christmas.

Aufgabe 6

a) 1. + e)/f) 2. + j) 3. + a) 4. + h) 5. + b) 6. + f)/i) 7. + c) 8. + d) 9. + g) 10. + e)

b)
1. Is this exercise difficult? / Is the water warm enough for swimming?
2. Can I get a bus to Chelsham?
3. Do you know the right answer?
4. Do you do your homework on the bus?
5. Have you seen my umbrella?
6. Is this exercise difficult? / Will he/she/your friend be staying for supper?
7. Does the hotel have / Has the hotel got a good garage?
8. Do my parents know where I am?
9. Has our son / Have you received our letter yet?
10. Is the water warm enough for swimming?

Aufgabe 7

1. My father asked me who **had left** the front door open.
2. She wants to know what we **are doing** / I **am doing** here.
3. His friend asked her how much money she **had (got)**.
4. The reporter requested information about how many prisoners **had escaped** before the prison staff **had found** the hole.
5. He wants to know when the football match **took** place.
6. The motorist asked the mechanic how soon he/she **could** repair his car.
7. Our youth leader wanted to know what **had happened** to John.
8. One of the tourists has just asked me how far Reading **is** from London.
9. The child asked his mother where flies **went** in the winter.
10. The police officer asked me what I **had done** after I **had left** the hotel.

Aufgabe 8

2. The mum **asked** her son **to wake up, and asked him** what the matter **was** with him.
3. Kieran **said** he **loved** French wine, and **asked** Peter **to pass him** the bottle.
4. Peter **asked if/whether** Marc **liked** wine too, and **suggested that they should offer** / **suggested offering** him some.
5. The teacher **told** his/her student to pay attention **and said that he/she had to** tell him/her everything twice.
6. Tania **ordered/commanded** her dog Robin **to come to her, asked/asking him** where **he had got** those sausages and **said/saying that he was** a bad dog.
7. The manager of the firm **asked** the project manager **if she was** Janet Smith. **When she said she was, he asked her to come** in and **sit** down. **Then he offered her** a coffee / **asked her if she wanted** a coffee.
8. Anna **told** her boyfriend Malek **that she had been** surprised not to see **him** at Phil's party. **She asked him** where **he had been the previous night, warning him** / **and warned him to tell her** the truth.
9. Oliver **suggested that we should wait** / **suggested waiting** a few minutes longer. **He told me he had** no idea where the others **had** got to, **and asked me whether I thought** they **were** lost.
10. The driving instructor **told** my brother **to stop, said** / **saying he hadn't seen** a red light **and asked/asking why he/she couldn't drive** more carefully.
11. My teacher **suggested that we should finish** / **suggested finishing** this exercise and **have/having** a break. **I said that was** a good idea.

6 Partizipien – Gerundium – Infinitiv

Aufgabe 1

1. interested in; interesting 2. frightening; frightened of 3. boiling; boiled 4. falling; fallen 5. booked; booking 6. terrified; terrifying 7. worn

Aufgabe 2

many people **living** in London – Cockney was the dialect **spoken** by people **born** in the East End – the church bells of St Mary-le-Bow (**known** as Bow Bells) – Foreigners **listening** to a real Cockney – A Cockney **saying**, … – Cockneys **educated** at grammar schools – someone less well **educated**

Aufgabe 3

2. The man **standing** 3. The one **wearing** 4. The one **dressed** 5. the man **wanted** by 6. the man **living** in 7. that bank **situated** 8. the one **invited** to 9. one of the men **working** at 10. a Scottish name **beginning** with Mac 11. that chain of restaurants **selling**

Aufgabe 4

2. The money **lying/found** in the suitcase was stolen from Lloyds Bank. *or*: The money **stolen** from Lloyds Bank was found in a suitcase.
3. The girl **sitting** on the bench is reading a book. *or*: The girl **reading** a book is sitting on a bench.
4. The letter **posted** on 12 August is lying on the desk. *or*: The letter **lying** on the desk was posted on 12 August.
5. The car **parked** in front of the house is from Great Britain. *or*: The car **registered** in Great Britain is / was parked in front of the house.
6. The languages **spoken** here are English, French and German.
7. The Queen is the woman **going** shopping at Harrods / into the store. *or*: The woman **going** shopping at Harrods / into the store is the Queen.
8. The woman **being interviewed** is the actress Jane Jones. *or*: The actress Jane Jones is the woman **being interviewed**.
9. "Hamlet" is the play **being put on** / **performed** at this theatre. *or*: The play **being put on** / **performed** at this theatre is "Hamlet".

Aufgabe 5

1. **Walking** across the room, I shut the door.
2. **Having listened** to the new song, we went out for a hamburger.
3. **Not knowing** the way, he asked a passerby.
4. *No change.*
5. Unless **taught** English properly, they will not be able to get good jobs abroad.
6. **When leaving** the train, passengers should take all their luggage with them.
7. Stay calm if **stopped** by a police officer.
8. Though **made** in Korea, this car is still very good.
9. *No change.*
10. **Walking** into the room, the headteacher sat down at the teacher's table.
11. *No change. or*: She had no worries until **told to leave** the country within 48 hours.
12. John went to Oxford after **getting** / **having got** four A's in his A-levels.

Aufgabe 6

1. **Shutting** the door, he sat down.
2. **Having passed** my driving test, I bought a car.
3. She sat in the bath **reading** a newspaper. – (**While**) **Sitting** in the bath she read a newspaper.
4. **Not wanting** to go, we stayed at home.
5. **Not having learnt** French at school, I wasn't able to read the letter.
6. My friend fell asleep (**while**) **watching** TV.
7. **Not living** in the area, she could not help me.
8. Our dog ran off, **having bitten** the postman.
   or: **Having bitten** the postman, our dog ran off.
9. **Being** foreigners, they had to learn English.
10. **Walking** to school, I learn ten English words on the way.
    or: I walk to school **learning** ten English words on the way.

Aufgabe 7

2. She just sat there **watching** TV.
3. The children went **running** down to the beach.
4. The police officers just stood there **waiting** for orders.
5. The food remained **untouched**.
6. He spends a lot of time **dancing** at discos.
7. The farmer caught two campers **camping** in his field without permission.
8. They have wasted a lot of time **playing** football at the weekends.
9. The sailor lay on the grass **asleep**. *or*: The sailor lay **asleep** on the grass.
10. They spent a lot of time **sunbathing**.
11. I can't stand here all day **waiting** for you! *or*: I can't stand here **waiting** for you all day!

Aufgabe 8

Einige Lösungsvorschläge:

I saw/watched several people **waiting** for the bus.
I saw/watched a street musician **playing** near the Underground.
I saw/watched several people **looking** in the shop windows.
I watched the traffic **driving** up and down.
I listened to a street musician **playing** near the Underground.
I heard several people **speaking** German.
I heard a police car **going** to an emergency.
I heard a plane **take off**.
I felt the hot sun **warming** the back of my neck.
I felt a hand **touch** my shoulder. It was my good friend Bob …

Aufgabe 9

Gerund:

I like **living** in the big city. – **Working** as an archaeologist must be fun. – I wouldn't mind **studying** archaeology – I love **walking** around the streets of London – streets which you can only reach by **walking** through narrow alleys – I have got used to **hearing** the sound of traffic – but **living** near the centre of a city – I must stop **writing** now and start **doing** my homework. – I look forward to **seeing** you at Christmas.

Present participle:

London is a **living** museum! – **Sitting** on the upper deck of a bus – the high wooden fence **surrounding** a big building site. – As well as **building** workers – students **looking** for Roman remains – The mist **rising** from the lakes – I would find myself **writing** about a big city – But after **living** in London for nearly four weeks – the sound of traffic **travelling** through the city – **Waking** up at night – makes life so much more **interesting**

Progressive form:

I've been **living** in Central London

Aufgabe 10

1. Swimming is one of my hobbies.
2. I like swimming in the sea.
3. I soon got used to swimming in salt water.
4. Swimming in a swimming pool is not as nice.
5. I don't mind going to the/an open-air swimming pool at the weekend(s).
6. My brother doesn't mind me/my going without him.
7. Collecting old records is his favourite hobby.
8. He finances/pays for his hobby by delivering newspapers.
9. My mum doesn't like him/his having to deliver newspapers in bad weather.
10. She is looking forward to him/his starting a proper job soon.

Aufgabe 11

1. to remember; living
2. moving
3. to ask
4. shopping
5. finding
6. asking
7. to talk
8. talking; telling
9. leaving
10. to live
11. to mention
12. to say

7 Das Passiv

Aufgabe 1

2. we will be met at the airport. 3. are opened. 4. rooms were booked 5. can be taken 6. are made on Malta. 7. were picked up 8. are visited 9. A coach trip can be taken 10. may/can not be booked 11. has been arranged

Aufgabe 2

2. is understood 3. is real English spoken? 4. tourists are disliked 5. was stolen 6. has been cleaned 7. hadn't been made 8. I am/we are liked

Aufgabe 3

1. A heavily-armed police riot squad **broke up** a peaceful demonstration in Trafalgar Square yesterday.
2. Angry police officers **arrested** several (peaceful) demonstrators.
3. After the riot squad **had been called**, probably by unnamed police informers,
4. armour-plated police vehicles **brought** about twenty police officers in riot gear to Trafalgar Square.
5. Bullying police officers **ordered** Jessica Davies, the leader of the demonstration, to ask her fellow demonstrators to go home.
6. Angry police armed with heavy sticks **took** one or two demonstrators to Marlborough Street police station. Police **kept** them there overnight because they refused to give their names.
7. Ms Catherine Binyon, chairperson of PEACE NOW, **has not yet been released**.
8. During the past few months our peaceful organisation **has held** four demonstrations.

Aufgabe 4

1. Industrial waste **is being discharged** into the river.
2. Rubbish **is being dumped** in the woods/forests.
3. Private cars **are not being used** efficiently.
4. Valuable raw materials **are being thrown** away.
5. Public transport **is not being used** enough.
6. A new hypermarket with a huge car park **is being built**.
7. Railway stations **are being closed**. / This railway station **is being closed** on 1st August.
8. Gas-guzzlers **are** still **being developed**.
9. Old paper and cardboard boxes **are not being recycled**.
10. Cigarette advertising **is** (still) **not being banned**.

Aufgabe 5

Nothing **is being done** about air pollution (by the present Government). Two new by-passes and another twenty miles of motorway **are being built** in my constituency alone! Last year they promised to halt construction of a nuclear power station which **was being planned**, but nothing **has been done**, and land near the River Don **is** already **being surveyed** in preparation for construction of this power station which **is** not **wanted**! The rivers in this beautiful part of Great Britain **are** still **being polluted**. Last year chemicals factories **were** still **being expanded** even though an enquiry into chemical pollution **had been promised**!

Aufgabe 6

Einige Lösungsvorschläge:

1. This book **was written** by a famous author / an Englishman.
2. Thatched houses **are not built** in Britain very often.
3. Live music **is** often **played** / **is being played** in this pub.
4. Good sandwiches **are made** / **sold** in this snack bar.
5. Excellent fruit **is grown** by these farmers / on this farm.
6. Gas-guzzlers **are/were** still **being built** / **made** by some car companies / **are** still **not banned** by the government.
7. The environment **is** still **being polluted** with chemicals / by some firms.
8. Young people **are (being) trained** as doctors.
9. Many souvenirs **are made** / **sold** here every year.
10. Spanish **is spoken** in Spain / many countries of South and Central America.

Aufgabe 7

1. More industrial waste **is being dumped** in our rivers than ever before
2. Prince William **was being followed** by 10 photographers yesterday
3. The Nobel peace prize **has been awarded** to a dog!
4. A famous film star **is being divorced** by her fifth husband
5. Good marks **have been "sold"** to pupils (by a teacher) for years
6. Foreign aid money **was being spent** on arms
7. Drugs **were taken** by champion runner
8. Traffic in northern Scotland **is being stopped** by 3 metres of snow
9. Baby seals **have been killed** again (by hunters)
10. Pop star Rihanna's next concert **will be cancelled**
11. A dog **is bitten** by a man
12. Many parts of Britain **are being flooded** (by heavy rain)

Aufgabe 8

1. Plenty **is being done**!
2. The problem **is being looked into** at this very moment!
3. I don't care what **is being worked on** by your cousin's firm!
4. A traffic-free zone **will/is going to be set up** as soon as
5. More people **are knocked down** and injured
6. who **would be locked up**!
7. You mean this matter **has been / was talked about** at a meeting
8. the matter **was brought up** at the end of the meeting
9. I think the pavements **are being obstructed** by all those cars!
10. It's not a bigger car park that **is needed**
11. Bikes can't **be towed away**!
12. But bikes have to **be chained up**! … Thirty bikes **have been stolen** already this year!

Aufgabe 9

2. **I was handed** the note.
3. **I have** never **been offered** a ride in her car!
4. **Weren't you sent** an invitation to his party?
5. **Haven't you been taught** to say "please" if you want something?
6. **You won't be told** the truth.
7. **We are being denied** our basic rights!
8. **I was being given** an injection when the lights went out.
9. **She is going to be awarded** first prize in the photographic competition.
10. **I haven't been shown** the photos yet.
11. **This bike wasn't stolen. It was sold** to me.
12. **She was promised** a new skateboard for Christmas.
13. **I have been left** £5,000 by my great-grandfather / in my great-grandfather's will.

Aufgabe 10

1. This parcel **was delivered** to the wrong address.
2. This problem **can't be explained** to people who know nothing about cricket.
3. They **have not been introduced** to the President yet.
4. The scenery **can** only **be described** to you with the help of these photos.
5. The following solution **is proposed** to you.
6. After the experiment **had been demonstrated** (to the students), the laboratory was full of smoke.
7. The results of the elections **were announced** to the angry crowd.
8. Nothing **was said** about this to me.
9. Clothes **are being distributed** to the refugees.
10. An alternative **was suggested** to the worried workers.

Aufgabe 11

1. We **had been told** that our bank was robbery-proof.
2. The alarm system **was said to be** perfect. …
3. The bank's security arrangements **are** now **felt to have been** inadequate.
4. The robbers **are believed to have been hiding** in the bank all night. We **were surprised** when we arrived for work.
5. We **were told to put up** our hands.
6. Then we **were made to lie** down on the floor.
7. The gang **is supposed to be** the same one that robbed the National Westminster Bank in Croydon last month.
8. These men **are known to be** dangerous criminals!
9. We **were told** not to move for ten minutes.
10. Other crooks **were said to be** outside, watching in case the alarm **was given**.
11. The robbers **were seen to leave** (the bank) in a fast car.
12. When they had gone the manager, Mr Simms, **was found to have had** a mild heart attack!

8 Modale Hilfsverben

Aufgabe 1

List 1 – Modal auxiliaries:

This Evacuation Order **must** be observed – (persons) **should** apply to the Commanding Officer – who **may** be able to help. – Residents **must** take all their furniture – No exceptions **can** be made – The general public **may** only visit – people **must not** leave the roads – because they **might** be injured – that the Army **ought to** keep its promise and **should** return Imber to the people

List 2 – Substitutes:

Imber **is to be** evacuated on 1st December 1943. – Any persons who **are not able to** find accommodation – no one **will be allowed to** return – Residents **will be able to** return – the last 150 residents … **had to** leave their homes – They **were allowed to** take their possessions – but **were forbidden** (= not allowed) to return to the village – only St Giles Church … and a few buildings **have been allowed** to remain

List 3 – Other tense-forming auxiliaries:

NOTICE **is** hereby given … – From 2nd December 1943, all roads … **will** be CLOSED … – No exceptions **can** be made to this Order, which **is** issued in the interests of National Security. – They … **were** forbidden to return to the village.

Aufgabe 2

1. Do we have
2. needn't
3. mustn't
4. had; ll/will have
5. has/will have/is having
6. 've/have had
7. have you had
8. needn't
9. must

Aufgabe 3

1. be able to
2. has never had
3. were able to
4. have never been able to
5. to be able to
6. will have to
7. to be able to
8. would be able to

9. hadn't been able to
10. can't/haven't been able to
11. will have to

Aufgabe 4

1. be allowed to
2. be allowed to
3. may not
4. may not
5. was allowed to
6. may
7. 'll be allowed to
8. Were you allowed to
9. weren't allowed to
10. May
11. Might
12. might
13. may
14. might
15. may/might

Aufgabe 5

1. **May** I borrow your book?
2. **Might** I possibly use your/your dad's computer?
3. I think this £5 note **may** be a forgery.
4. I think you **might** be too young to watch the horror film with me.
5. We **may** take/have a holiday in Spain next year.
6. If we had more money we **might** take/have a holiday on Hawaii.
7. You **may** not borrow my car!
8. I don't think we **will be allowed to** go alone.
9. If my brother went with us I think I **would be allowed to** go to the concert.
10. You **may** be right.
11. It **might** be right/wrong.
12. At home I'**ve** always **been allowed to** watch my favourite TV programme!

Aufgabe 6

1. **Shall we go** for a bike ride in the country?
2. Perhaps we **should take** our coats with us.
3. Perhaps we **oughtn't to** / **shouldn't go** too far.
4. The little lake on the edge of the forest **is said to be good for swimming**.
5. Hey! You **oughtn't to** / **shouldn't cycle** on the left-hand side!
6. I **ought to know** that by now!
7. It**'s supposed** / **said to be** haunted.
8. **Shall we have** a look around?
9. That sign means nobody **is supposed** to go inside the house.
10. Perhaps we **oughtn't to** / **shouldn't** / we'**d better not go** in, then.
11. Yes, if **anyone**/**someone were to see** us we might get into trouble.
12. I think we **should** / **ought to** / we'**d better go** home before it gets dark.

Aufgabe 7

1. **Do** you **wish**/**want to** speak to me, Mr Richards?
2. Oh, Jana! Yes. I **was going** / **wanted** / **intended to** phone you this morning.
3. I **was going to** / **wanted to** ask you if you would like to take part in our class trip.
4. I really **intended** / **meant to** stay at home at the weekend.
5. My aunt **wants** / **is going** / **intends** / (**means**) **to** visit us.
6. They **wanted** / **intended to** see the film, but did not **want** / **intend to** queue for tickets.
7. What **do you intend** / **are you going to** do with the money?
8. I'**m going to** buy a mountain bike.
9. I'**ve** always **wanted to** have a mountain bike.

9 Relativsätze

Aufgabe 1

Lösungsvorschläge:

2. A toaster is a device **which/that is used / you use for making toast**.
3. A winner is a person **who/that wins a prize, a race, etc**.
4. Dinner is a meal **which/that you eat / is eaten in the evening**.
5. A fridge is a device **which/that keeps food cool / which you find in most kitchens**.
6. A bike is a device **which/that you use to get to school on time**.
7. A manager is a person **who/that manages/runs a shop/company/business**.
8. A watch is a (kind of) small clock **which/that you wear on your arm**.
9. Soap is a thing/something **which/that you use when you wash / to wash with**.
10. Jam is a food **which/that you put on bread and butter / which you eat for breakfast**.
11. Commas are things/punctuation marks **which/that separate a main and subordinate clause** in German / that German grammar is very fond of.

Aufgabe 2

1. I saw the Harry Potter films first. Then Mum bought me all the books**, which were very expensive**.
2. He only bought cheap paperbacks. He didn't buy books **that/which were very expensive**.
3. I have two sisters. This is a photo of my sister **who/that is 16 years old**.
4. My friend Harry**, who is 16 years old,** lives in Bournemouth.
5. The woman **who/that teaches us** French is OK,
6. Mr Strickland**, who teaches us** German**,** is very strict.
7. Mum drives the car **which/that is in the garage**.
8. My dad uses his old bike**, which is in the garage** too.
9. "My girlfriend**, who has red hair,** lives next door to me."
10. "There's a girl **who/that has red hair** in my class at school."

Aufgabe 3

Bei den Pronomen, die in Klammern stehen, handelt es sich um Relativpronomen, die in der Umgangssprache oft weggelassen werden – aus der direkten „pronomenlosen" Berührung zwischen Haupt- und Relativsatz entsteht der so genannte *contact clause*.

2. Have you played the new game (**which/that**) I lent to your sister Caroline?
3. This is the boy (**who(m)/that**) I saw at the party last week.
4. Here's my new bike**, which** I got for my birthday.
5. This is Linda**, who(m)** we talked to at Jim's party.
6. They are the new group (**which/that**) you heard on the internet yesterday. (*Hier wäre auch „(who/whom)" möglich, da es sich bei einer Gruppe natürlich auch um Personen handelt.*)
7. John didn't see the car (**which/that**) the robbers escaped in.
8. We all know Mickey Mouse, (**who/whom**) Walt Disney invented.
9. I like milk chocolate**, which** you can buy all over the world.
10. Have you read Petra's email**, which** she sent two days ago?
11. You're the man (**who/whom/that**) I've been waiting for since lunchtime.
12. Here is my bike**, which** I left in the garden overnight.
13. He wrote to a Scottish girl (**who/whom/that**) he met in Spain last month.

Aufgabe 4

Je nachdem, ob du annimmst, der *British way of life* sei in **allen** Commonwealth-Ländern kritiklos übernommen worden oder nur in **bestimmten** Ländern, brauchst du das Komma im ersten Satz. Dir ist sicher klar, warum!

Rugby is a game **which/that** is extremely popular in Britain, France, Australia, South Africa, New Zealand and in fact many other Commonwealth countries in **which** the British way of life predominated. The game was 'invented' by a boy **who** was a pupil at Rugby School in 1823. He was the first player **who** ("that" ist hier zwar möglich, ist aber vor einem eingekapselten Nebensatz unüblich), during a normal game of football, in **which** players normally only kicked the ball, picked up the ball, **which** in those days was not perfectly round but slightly oval as it still is in rugby and American football today, and ran with it.
There are two types of rugby: Rugby Union**, which** is an amateur sport played at schools, and Rugby League, a professional sport (**which/that**) many people watch every Saturday in the North of England. There are fifteen players in a Rugby Union team and only thirteen in a Rugby League team. International rugby matches**, which** the French and Welsh enjoy more than soccer matches, are played under Rugby Union rules and are well attended by thousands of fans**, who** often travel long distances to see the games.
The 'inventor' of the game, William Webb Ellis**, who(m)** few people know by name, became a clergyman in later life and died in 1872. Rugby is also a game (**which/that**) women enjoy playing. Most men's teams also have a women's team **which/that** play most Saturdays.

Aufgabe 5

Three students meet on the first day at university.

1. One of them is Kevin**, whose** friend Nils has just arrived from Germany.
2. Nils is the German exchange student **whose** parents invited Kevin to stay during the summer vacation.
3. Kevin's best friend John is standing in front of the noticeboard in the corridor**, whose** notices / **the notices of which** are usually very interesting.
4. Kevin introduces his two friends to each other. "This is John**, whose** parents are good friends of ours."
5. "John, this is Nils, my German friend **whose** parents I stayed with during the summer vacation."
6. "Hello, John. I'm the exchange student from Germany **whose** room is on the floor above yours."
7. "Pleased to meet you. Is that your car outside? The blue one **whose** windows / **the windows of which** are all open."
8. "Did I leave the windows open? It was so hot in town! I was stuck behind a long line of cars **whose** drivers / **the drivers of which** all seemed to be asleep!"
9. "Should I go downstairs and shut the windows? Are there many car thieves on the campus?" – "Last term thieves stole several cars **whose** owners / **the owners of which** had forgotten to lock them!"
10. "I'll go down and lock my car right away." But suddenly the three students heard a voice from a loudspeaker in the corridor: "Will the owner of the blue car, German registration number HN-LS 317, **whose** windows are open and **whose** doors are unlocked / **the windows of which** are open and **the doors of which** are unlocked, please come downstairs at once."

Aufgabe 6

An old country railway station **which** the Council wanted to pull down has been saved at the last minute. The "Save our Station" campaign**, whose** leader / **the leader of which** is Robin Wilson, talked to our reporter and said that experts had examined the part of the building **whose** walls / **the walls of which** the council had said were unsafe. The experts said that the walls only needed a few simple repairs, **which** any local builder could do. The money **which/that** had been given by supporters of the campaign / (**which/that**) supporters of the campaign had given was/would be almost enough for the repairs. Many people heard about the campaign, **which** was publicised by local radio stations. They criticised the Council, **whose** decision / **the decision of which** was not widely publicised. Robin Wilson is now looking for volunteers **who/that** can come and help do the necessary repair work, **which** will take about four weeks. The chairman of the Council committee **who** (*„that" könnte hier heißen, dass das* ***Komitee*** *die Entscheidung gefällt hat: wenn die* ***Person*** *gemeint ist, sollte man „who" verwenden, um Verwechslungen zu vermeiden*) made the decision is very angry. Robin Williams, **who(m)** local people admire, got married last week. He met his wife, **who** comes from London, as a result of his campaign work. They are both dynamic people **who(m)/that** (*Weglassung hier aus Betonungsgründen nicht zu empfehlen*) the Council chairman dislikes intensely.

Aufgabe 7

2. She said she couldn't help me**, which** was just an excuse.
3. He arrived half an hour late**, which** was very impolite of him.
4. My sister watches TV a lot**, which** is not good for her.
5. Last week I went to a family wedding**, which** I usually hate!
6. All my cousins were there**, which** made the wedding more fun.
7. Even my great-grandmother was there**, which** astonished everyone.
8. The old lady is 99 years old**, which** makes her the oldest member of our family.
9. When my father saw my last school report, he got very angry**, which** didn't surprise me.
10. I had bad marks in most subjects**, which** I couldn't explain.
11. Luckily I had a 2 in English**, which** surprised my father.
12. He told me his best mark for English at school had been a 3**, which** shocked me.
13. His marks in other subjects had been bad too**, which** I didn't know!

Aufgabe 8

1. This is the book which I was telling you about. I read it in three days**,** which is very fast for me! It's a story about a pop group which started at our school.
2. Tom suggested a party**,** which I thought was a good idea. Then Jenny suggested a barbecue**,** which sounded like an even better idea. She said she had plenty of food left from the barbecue which they had had at the weekend.
3. He said he played the guitar in a pop group which was very good. His sister said that she was a singer in the same group**,** which is nonsense. My friend John told me it was a true story**,** which I didn't believe. But he has often told me stories which I didn't believe.

Aufgabe 9

2. I find it hard to believe **what he tells me**.
3. **What** is important is to learn ten new words a day.
4. Tell me something about **what your mum does**.
5. **What he did** was hard to explain.
6. I watched him carefully but couldn't observe **what he did** exactly.
7. **What they suggested** was out of the question.
8. Three strong men are **what is needed** to move this piano.
9. A big portion of fish and chips is precisely **what I want/wish**.
10. **What you think** is not important. **What you do** is.
11. **What** goes on at my school would surprise you!

Quellennachweis

Zeichnungen: Christa Janik, Leinfelden-Echterdingen: S. 18, 41, 54, 72, 78, 93, 110, 111;
Lars Benecke, Hannover: S. 99
Bildnachweis: Adobe Stock, Dublin: S. 32.1 gazanfer, S. 32.2 Winyou, S. 32.3 Drazen, S. 32.4 Köpenicker, S. 32.5 TATIANA, S. 32.6 Тарас Нагирняк, S. 32.7 undrey, S. 32.8 fizkes, S. 32.9 Patrick Foto, S. 48 KVN1777, S. 49.3 Андрей Михайлов, S. 49.4 наталья саксонова, S. 49.5 happy_lark, S. 49.6 Chanwit, S. 49.7 MP2, S. 65.1 THANANIT, S. 65.2 kytalpa, S. 65.3 makibestphoto, S. 65.5 frank11, S. 65.6 seanlockephotography, S. 65.7 wip-studio; Fotolia, New York: S. 65.8 frizio; Getty Images, München: S. 49.1 SimplyCreativePhotography, S. 49.2 RapidEye, S. 65.4 urbancow, S. 65.9 Image Source

Der Verlag hat sich nach bestem Wissen und Gewissen bemüht, alle Inhaber von Urheberrechten an Texten und Abbildungen zu diesem Werk ausfindig zu machen. Sollte das in irgendeinem Fall nicht korrekt geschehen sein, bitten wir um Entschuldigung und bieten an, gegebenenfalls in einer nachfolgenden Auflage einen korrigierten Quellennachweis zu bringen.

Stichwortverzeichnis